DRAMA THAT DELIVERS

DRAMA THAT DELIVERS
Real-Life Problems, Students' Solutions

Nancy Duffy Hery

1996
TEACHER IDEAS PRESS
A Division of
Libraries Unlimited, Inc.
Englewood, Colorado

To my Mom and Dad,
who taught me that a sense of humor and a little hard work
never hurt anyone.
To my husband
David
and my children Katie and Duffy.
Thanks for all the encouragement and suggestions.

Copyright © 1996 Nancy Duffy Hery
All Rights Reserved
Printed in the United States of America

TEACHER IDEAS PRESS
A Division of
LIBRARIES UNLIMITED, INC.
P.O. Box 6633
Englewood, CO 80155-6633
1-800-237-6124

Constance Hardesty, *Project Editor*
Pamela J. Getchell, *Design and Layout*

Library of Congress Cataloging-in-Publication Data

Hery, Nancy Duffy, 1955-
    Drama that delivers : real-life problems, students' solutions /
Nancy Duffy Hery.
        xi, 113 p. 22x28 cm.
        Includes bibliographical references.
        ISBN 1-56308-429-5
        1. Group guidance in education.   2. Group guidance of teenagers.
    3. Drama in education.   4. Role playing.   I. Title.
    LB1027.5.H47   1996
        371.4'6--dc20
                                            96-24641
                                            CIP

CONTENTS

 # PREFACE

The use of a variety of teaching strategies within a classroom will help more students learn effectively. Problem solving, logical thinking, reasoning, and critical thinking are all important skills whose use is encouraged throughout these chapters. By performing the plays and working through the activities in this book, students will develop skills to make healthy choices.

One of the most popular and successful ways to teach and talk about sensitive issues is through drama and role playing. This method has been used for years by psychologists and counselors. I have found it to be most successful with middle-school children.

A study of 355 seventh-grade students was conducted concerning seven learning strategies. The student ratings for the strategies concluded that students felt they learned and enjoyed the most in the classes that involved simulations, games, problem solving, and discussion (Theobold, 1995). All of these learning strategies are used in each chapter.

Adolescents have a hard time accepting all the changes in their lives, and they generally go through many ups and downs daily. They want to take responsibility for their own lives but sometimes don't feel ready. Students from all walks of life and all abilities enjoy stepping out of character and reading about someone else who has problems such as theirs.

I hope that you will enjoy incorporating these plays into your lessons as much as I have. When students can relate to what you are teaching, they will become excited about learning.

REFERENCE

Theobold, Margaret A. "What Students Say About Common Teaching Practices." *Columbus, Ohio, Middle School Journal,* 1995.

ACKNOWLEDGMENTS

Many people helped and encouraged me to write this book, but the main reason I wrote this was for my students. I would like to thank my students from Pine Forest and Discovery Middle School and my children who taught me, as I taught them. My love for these students and my own children has always encouraged me to keep teaching.

I want to express my sincere thanks to my fellow teachers, who have inspired me and helped with the development of this text. Middle school teachers are among the most dedicated people, and if I leave anyone out, it's not because I don't appreciate you. Thank you for sharing your expertise Jamie Wells, my best friend and coworker; you have taught me more about life than teaching. Thanks for putting up with me and for your ideas, Dianne LeBruto, Patricia Franklin, Jeanne Morgan, Elaine Brindley, Tina Petro, and Gail Lennon. Bouncing ideas, problems, and laughter off of each other has made this book possible. You're the best!

I want to thank my old and dear friends from Duluth, Minnesota. They had to put up with me as I wrote plays as a child. Thanks to my sister Jeanne, and friends Janelle, Suzee, Pam, Mary, Bonnie, and Rose.

Lastly, thanks for starring in my first play, John. Your humor and wit will truly be missed by your family and friends. I'm sorry I couldn't reach you in time.

INTRODUCTION

Personal and social issues can often be difficult subjects to discuss in the classroom. An effective way to explore these issues is through drama. When a student feels ownership in a problem through role playing, that problem suddenly becomes more relevant.

As a technique, having students perform plays is very effective in teaching about social and personal issues. Through drama, one can create imaginary situations and environments, which in turn can provide a new awareness for the student.

When students act as another person, they aren't threatened by the problem because it doesn't seem as personal as it would in real life. Suddenly students have a chance to role play different characters, especially those they don't identify with. A simulated experience can affect one's judgment, provide insight into a problem, and clarify one's understanding of a situation.

Because my students enjoyed reading and acting in plays, I went on a search for plays in the library dealing with social and personal issues. I couldn't find many, and those that I did find had only five to six characters. What could I do to bring this interesting teaching method into my classroom in a way that would involve more students? I decided the best thing to do was to write my own plays.

Each chapter is written in a way that flows best for the teacher and the student. First, information about the subject is provided, then the play, followed by questions for discussion, and a few ideas that can be used as springboards to develop activities that involve critical thinking, decision making, and group participation. Higher-order thinking skills are used during the discussion that follows each play. Students will reason, as well as question, why the characters in the play reacted as they did.

The plays are designed to enhance existing curriculum. The ideas for activities work well as enhancement or to entice students. Some of the suggestions do not deal directly with the specific topic of the play they follow but rather with the general subject involved in each drama. For example, some of the ideas following the play *You Can Never Be Too Thin* (chapter 4) deal with nutrition rather than eating disorders; that is because eating disorders are often discussed within the larger context of the nutrition portion of the health curriculum.

After reading one play, students will readily volunteer to read the next one. I hope that your students enjoy these plays as much as mine have.

DRAMA

1

Alcoholism in the Family

When someone abuses alcohol, everyone in that person's family is affected. Alcoholics not only destroy themselves, they also hurt everyone around them. For that reason, alcoholism is called a family illness.

A person can become addicted both mentally and physically to alcohol. When this occurs, the problem is considered a disease called alcoholism. This disease can damage the brain and body organs and affect how people deal with their anger and make judgments. In the final stages of alcoholism, the body has a physical need for alcohol. Alcoholics cannot function without a drink. In order to have fun, relax, or go to work, they feel they must have a drink first.

How can a family member help someone who has an alcohol problem? Because most alcoholics deny they have a problem, helping is difficult. The Children of Alcoholics Foundation estimates there are 7 million children under the age of 18 living with an alcoholic parent. These children can do little for their parents because alcoholics do not want to believe they have a problem and will not appreciate help, even from their own children.

The following suggestions may help children of alcoholics:

1. Take control of your own life and do not feel responsible for the drinkers' problems. Let the drinkers fail.

2. Talk to your counselor about joining a support group at school. Many schools offer self-help groups.

3. Call a local chapter of Alateen. This group helps children of alcoholic parents. The number for this organization should be listed in the local telephone directory.

4. Check out books in the local or school library about other children with the same problem. These stories will make students see that their parents' alcoholism isn't their fault and that there are many other people out there with the same

problem. See the recommended readings section of this chapter for specific titles.

5. Encourage other relatives and friends of the alcoholic to attend Al-Anon or Alateen. Al-Anon is a place for teens, family members, and friends of all ages. Alateen is a place for teens with alcoholic family members to share their problems with peers.

Children of alcoholics must take on many roles in the family. These roles are often a means of survival for the child. The responsible child is often the oldest and takes care of the other children and the household. The troublemaker won't put up with the alcoholic parent. This child often starts drinking at an early age. Some children "suffer in silence" and never let anyone know there is a problem. This child is the martyr. Martyrs often have to lie to keep the secret. The peacemaker is the child who will do anything to keep peace in the family. This child doesn't want to hear shouting or screaming and sometimes uses humor to diffuse situations.

The guilt and shame children feel about having an alcoholic in the family tends to isolate them. They won't allow others to come over to their house for fear they will see the alcoholic in a drunken stupor. In order to deny what is going on, they often lie to peers, teachers, and friends.

The following play, *Boy, I Wish Those Were My Parents*, addresses many of these situations. The play shows how difficult life is for the children of an alcoholic. Students will have the opportunity to see that alcoholism affects not only the immediate family, but also friends and neighbors. This drama also presents students with an opportunity to see how they can be a positive influence in helping others who live in this devastating situation.

This play will help many students recognize that other children have the same problems they do. Common problems and experiences will help many of the children overcome their frustration. When given an opportunity to read about someone in the same situation they are in, students find the problem easier to discuss. The main goal is for them to see that it is OK to receive outside help and that they are not alone.

BOY, I WISH THOSE WERE MY PARENTS

Nancy Duffy Hery

Alcoholism is a disease that can affect an entire family. In some cases, it runs in families. This play will discuss the problem and how it is often hidden, with the family taking on all the responsibility for the alcoholic.

Characters:

Joan	Rose	Andre
Dennis	Helen	Aeisha
Billy	Patrick	Linda
Dad	Joseph	Lee
Mom		

Scene 1   Joan, Billy, and Dennis are outside on the front porch.

Joan:
Hey, Dennis, Billy . . . Why are you two goofs standing out on the front steps in the rain? Did you forget your key again?

Dennis:
We didn't forget our key. Mom and Dad are screaming at each other again and we don't feel like going in and getting yelled at. I think Dad is really drunk this time.

Billy:
I'm afraid to go in. Last time he started imagining that I wanted to fight him and I hardly even said a word.

Joan:
We have to go in there. Who else will help Mom when he starts swinging at her and she starts to cry? Then he even gets worse. Come on.

Scene 2   Joan, Billy, and Dennis join Mom and Dad in the kitchen.

Joan:
Hi Mom, Dad . . . we're home.

Dad:
Oh look who's here. Miss smart aleck herself. She finally has decided that she lives here and can do some work around here. I can't believe you haven't quit school yet.

Joan:
Dad, why are you being so cruel to me?

Dad:
Shut up when I'm talking to you. What, hasn't anyone given you a look yet? You're loose just like your Mother . . . after all the guys.

Mom:
Stop it, John. Leave the kids out of this.

Dad:
This is my house and I'll say what I like around here. I am sick of these brats running this house. I give them everything they need and all I get is back talk.

Billy:
Dad, you don't mean what you're saying. Why don't you go lie down for awhile and sleep it off?

Dad:
Who do you think you're talking to, tough guy? Come on, tough guy. Show me what ya got. Or maybe you're some kind of sissy.

Billy:
Some day you will regret saying that to me.

Dad:
That's it. Come here, little sissy, and let's duke it out right now.

Billy:
I'm leaving. I'm not going to deal with a drunk.

Mom:
Stop it, both of you!

Dad:
Oh sure, pamper them. See how these brats talk to me? Hey, get back here. I'm talking to you. Don't leave the room when I'm talking. You all think your Dad is some big dumb jerk.

Joan:
We didn't say that Dad. We love you. Please stop screaming.

Dad:
This is my house, and I'll scream if I want to. Who do you think you are? I'm in charge here.

Billy:
Dad, when are you going to get help? We are sick of covering for you all the time. You have a drinking problem.

Dad:
Don't get smart with me. (*slaps Billy across the face*)

Dennis:
Stop it, Dad! Billy is right, you need help.

Dad: (*screaming*)
That's it! I'm going down the street, and when I get back I expect to see some attitude changes.

Mom:
Honey, don't leave. The kids didn't mean anything by what they said. Come on, let's have some supper and relax.

Dennis:
Dad, don't go, you've had too much to drink already. Come on, sit down and have dinner.

Dad:
Get out of my way, Momma's boy. You're useless. What's wrong with you? Where did I get such useless kids anyway?

Dad leaves the house and the family is standing in the kitchen. The phone is ringing.

Dennis:
Hello . . . just a minute. Joan, it's for you.

Joan:
OK, just a minute. (*whispers to Mom*) Mom, we have got to talk about this. We need to get Dad involved in Alcoholics Anonymous. He's ruining himself and our family.

Mom:
Oh, he'll be fine. He just needs to sleep it off. He had a hard day at work. He doesn't mean all those awful things he says to you. It's the liquor talking and he gets mean.

Dennis:
Joan! Get the phone!

Joan:
Oh, yeah, OK . . . Hello.

Rose:
Hi Joan. Do you need a ride to the game? I'm so glad you're feeling better. We really need you in this game as a starter.

Joan:
Well, to answer your first question, yes I'll be there. But, no I don't need a ride to the game. Thanks, anyway. You know how my family is. My Dad likes us to do everything together. It's kind of like a family night at my house, so after my Dad takes us to the game, we're all going out to dinner.

Rose:
You're so lucky. My Mom is really busy tonight, so she can only drop us off at the game and pick us up. That is so nice your Dad has the time for you.

Joan:
Yeah, my Dad wants to do so many family things together that sometimes I get tired of it.

Rose:
Well, I'll see you at the gym. Bye.

Joan:
See ya there.

Dennis:
Why do you always lie to your friends and pretend that everything is OK?

Billy:
You know what Mom always tells us. What happens in this house is only our business and stays behind closed doors.

Mom:
Dad is going through a rough time right now. When times are rough he tends to drink more.

Joan:
Mom, you always have an excuse for him. He hits you, hits us, screams at us and constantly tells us what lousy people we are. He blames everything on us, and I am sick of taking the blame for him getting drunk all the time.

Dennis:
Maybe it is our fault that he drinks. We might get on his nerves.

Mom:
Well, we'll pretend that this never happened when he gets home and maybe he'll be nicer to us.

Dennis:
Who are you trying to kid, Mom? I'm going over to spend the night at Paul's house. I'm not going to be here to get smacked for looking at him the wrong way.

Joan:
Come on, Mom. I have a game at 7. Why don't you come to the game? You never get to see me play.

Mom:
I can't. You know how your Dad thinks I'll be looking at other men if I go anywhere without him. You go on ahead and I'll wait for him here.

Dennis:
We hate leaving you home alone to face him.

Mom:
Just go on. I'll be sure he gets home safely and put him to bed. He needs some rest.

Billy:
I'm going to watch Joan's game. We'll hurry home before he gets here. Are you sure you're OK?

Mom:
I'm sure. He won't be home 'til late.

Joan:
We're not eating 'til after the game. Bye, Mom, I love you.

Mom:
I love you, too.

Joan, Billy, and Dennis exit. Mom is standing in the kitchen alone when the phone rings.

Mom:
Hello.

Helen:
Hi Dianne, how's it going? We missed you at bowling this week.

Mom:
Oh, you know how John is. He was able to get tickets to go to the new play in town and he wanted to take me and the family. He is always doing special things like that.

Helen:
Aren't you lucky to have such a great guy?

Mom:
I sure am. The play was wonderful.

Helen:
Well, listen, I also called to see if you wanted to go to aerobics together.

Mom:
I would love to, but John and I have made plans for a quiet evening together.

Helen:
Well, excuse me. How romantic. I'll catch you another time. See ya at work.

Mom:
Thanks for calling.

Scene 3 **The school gymnasium bleachers. Patrick, Joseph, Andre, Aeisha, Linda, and Lee are hanging around before the game. Joan approaches the group.**

Patrick:
Hey, here comes the star of the team.

Joseph:
I hope she didn't ruin her make-up getting here. Quick, someone get her a comb for her hair.

Joan: (*laughing*)
Shut up, Joe. You're jealous.

Andre:
He wishes Joan would pay a little attention to him.

Patrick:
Come on, Joseph, tell the truth. Go ahead and ask Joan out.

Joseph:
I would, but, first I have to get past her two brothers.

Aeisha:
Yeah, they'll kick your butt if you're not good to their sister.

Joan:
Will you guys stop it? You're embarrassing me.

Linda:
Hey, where's your parents, Joan? I thought you were riding with them.

Joan:
They're on their way. My brother and I decided to walk. They were stopping at the mall to surprise us with something.

Patrick:
Must be nice.

Lee:
Yeah, my parents always surprise me with something, like a nice new lawn mower to cut the grass with.

Andre:
Or how about a new washing machine? That's what our big surprise was last week.

Lee:
So, Joan, what do you think they're buying this time?

Aeisha:
Yeah, Joan, you're always bragging about all the new stuff your Dad gets for you.

Joan:
You never know what to expect.

Linda:
Hey, here comes the coach.

Joan exits. The rest of the group sits in the bleachers to watch the game.

Linda:
I wish my parents were like Joan's parents.

Andre:
I've never met them, but they seem too good to be true.

Lee:
Yeah, she talks about them like she worships them. You guys might think I'm crazy, but don't you think that it's funny that her parents never show up for anything at school? They are always going to come, but they never make it.

Joseph:
How do you know all of this?

Lee:
Because I've given her rides home before because they didn't show.

Linda:
Yeah, ya know, you might be right.

Andre:
Have you noticed how many days of school she misses?

Patrick:
I think you guys are nuts. Joan seems like the happiest girl in the world to me. She gets good grades and loves school.

Joseph:
Yeah, Joan brags about her parents all the time. I guess her Dad is a great guy.

Patrick:
If he is such a great guy how come we never see him?

Linda:
Do you think her parents have a problem? She always seems nervous when I go to pick her up. She never lets anyone into the house.

Andre:
Maybe her parents have a drinking or drug problem. If my parents were drinkers, I sure wouldn't tell anyone. It's embarrassing.

Lee:
Would you tell anyone if your parents were drunks or into drugs?

Linda:
No way. I would keep it a secret. And now that you mention it, I did drop by her house once to give her some homework and her Dad answered the door and he was pretty drunk.

Patrick:
Maybe that smiling face is just an act.

Joseph:
What can we do to help her if her parents do have problems?

Andre:
Listen, if her parents have problems, then the whole family has problems. I never told any of you this, but my Mom is a recovering alcoholic. We always covered for her, called in sick for her at work and pretended everything was great. Then when she hit rock bottom and lost her job she decided to go to an AA meeting, which is Alcoholics Anonymous. She hasn't had a drink in three years, but she needs to go to the meetings.

Linda:
Hey Andre, we're sorry. We didn't mean to make you feel bad. We didn't know.

Andre:
Actually, I'm kind of glad you know. It makes it easier on me not to feel bad about it. Sometimes I used to blame myself for my Mom's problems. I think I might talk to Joan after the game. Maybe if I explain my problem she might open up to me.

Linda:
She might be mad at you, but it's worth a try.

QUESTIONS FOR DISCUSSION

1. Why do families of alcoholics tend to lie for them and tell stories to cover up the problem?

2. How can Joan's friends help her without embarrassing her?

3. Why do you think Joan's mother stays with her husband and puts up with this?

4. Why does Joan lie to her friends?

5. Is alcoholism a family disease? How does it affect the whole family?

6. Why do alcoholics put others down all the time?

RECOMMENDED READINGS

Fiction

Cavana, Betty. *The Surfer and the City Girl.* New York: Westminster Press, 1981.

Fox, Paula. *Moonlight Man.* New York: Broadway Press, 1986.

Greene, Sheppard. *The Boy Who Drank Too Much.* New York: Dell, 1979.

Kropp, Paul. *Runaway.* New York: EMC, 1982.

Nonfiction

Fishman, Ross. *Alcohol and Alcoholism.* New York: Chelsea, 1987.

Grosshandler, Janet. *Coping with Alcohol Abuse.* New York: Rosen, 1990.

Knox, Jean. *Drinking, Driving, Drugs.* New York: Chelsea, 1988.

Porterfield, Kay Marie. *Coping with an Alcoholic.* New York: Rosen, 1990.

Ryerson, Eric. *When Your Parent Drinks Too Much.* New York: Warner, 1985.

Turk, Mary. *Facts About Alcohol and Tobacco.* New York: Crestwood House, 1988.

IDEAS FOR ACTIVITIES

Speakers

Speakers from Alateen and MADD (Mothers Against Drunk Driving) will talk to a class. Listings for these groups can be found in your local telephone directory. Addresses and telephone numbers for these organizations' national headquarters can be found in *The Encyclopedia of Associations* (Gale, annual).

Cooperative Groups

Students cut out advertisements for alcohol from magazines or a local newspaper. Students then write down their answers to the following questions: What is the ad trying to tell you? What type of people are in the ads and what are they doing? Do any of the ads show a family doing something together? How is the advertiser trying to convince you to buy alcohol?

Creative Activity

Students create a television announcement to tell the real facts about alcohol. The announcements are taped, and the best ones are aired during morning announcements.

Current Events

From the local newspaper, students cut out articles about accidents that involve drunk drivers. Post the articles on a bulletin board. The students compile and chart information about the ages of the victims, where and what time the accidents occurred, injuries suffered, and how many people were involved. Students follow up with a discussion of how the accidents could have been avoided.

Decision Making

Groups of five students are handed different scenarios involving drinking and decision making that the students themselves could encounter. Members of each group write their decisions and the consequences of those decisions on large sheets of paper, which they share with the rest of their group. Members of a group do not need to come to consensus, but may hold various opinions, which they share in the small group discussion.

Class Activity

In small groups students receive a large piece of butcher paper. On the paper each student writes 10 reasons why kids drink and 10 reasons why they should not drink. After the small groups make their lists, the class as a whole discusses each group's list of reasons and adds any additional reasons that come up during the class discussion.

Enrichment Activity

Students reflect on their lives and then write a paragraph or two describing the things that are most important to them and how drinking alcohol might affect any of these. Suggest they consider the effects of drinking by various people: themselves, a family member, or even strangers.

Entertainment Ideas

In small groups students write down 10 different ways to have a good time that don't cost money. Then they write down 10 ways to have a good time for under $10.

Nutrition

Young people rarely consider calories and nutrition when they drink. Give students two lists, one showing the number of calories of 10 alcoholic beverages, and the other showing the calories consumed in one hour by 10 activities. Have them match the activities and drinks to determine how long they would need to exercise to burn the calories from each drink.

In an extension of this activity, students research the nutritional value of alcoholic drinks, how the body metabolizes alcohol, what vitamins are lost in the process, and other related topics. Students present their findings to the class.

Community Activity

Throughout the area schools, have a poster contest or button contest that advocates avoiding alcohol. Students could ask local businesses to sponsor the event by providing prizes, by funding the reproduction of the winning entries, and by displaying the winning posters or distributing the winning buttons.

REFERENCES

Fishman, Ross. *Alcohol and Alcoholism.* New York: Chelsea, 1987.

Porterfield, Kay Marie. *Coping with an Alcoholic.* New York: Rosen, 1990.

Turk, Mary. *Facts About Alcohol and Tobacco.* New York: Crestwood House, 1988.

2
Suicide:
Teens in Trouble

All of us, at some time in our lives, have felt sad or lonely. This feeling of sadness can be brought on by a particular event, low self-esteem, a dysfunctional family, alcoholism or drugs, or a feeling that no one loves you. Sad times are normal for everyone. Sadness or despair that lingers for many weeks is called depression and is not normal. A person who experiences depression needs professional help.

Coping with depression and stress may be especially difficult for teenagers. They experience various problems that are difficult but that can be overcome. At a time in their lives when they are trying to fit in, teenagers may find additional stress too much for them. Teenagers must learn to cope with these problems in a positive manner. This may take some work, but it can be accomplished.

What are some events that cause young people to think about suicide? Breaking up with a boyfriend or girlfriend, not being a part of a group, appearance problems, drug or alcohol use, divorce in the family, the death of a close friend or family member, and the need to be successful in athletics or academics are just a few of the reasons that young people have given for why they have considered suicide. Along with these specific problems, suicidal teenagers have the feeling that things will never get better.

A teenager with extreme emotional pain may consider suicide. The warning signs of suicide are:

- Changes in personality or mood
- Withdrawal from friends and activities
- Drug and alcohol abuse
- Taking unusual risks
- Talk or thoughts of suicide or death
- A previous suicide attempt

17

- A parent or relative who committed suicide

- Giving away prized possessions

- Being a victim of sexual abuse

Teenagers want to live. They want help. If you suspect someone needs your help, there are many steps to take.

The following are a few places you can go for help or can recommend to a student you suspect is in danger of committing suicide:

- Teen hot lines

- Crisis centers

- Teachers, counselors

- Ministers, rabbis, or any church member

- Peer counseling groups at school

- SAFE teams at school

- Friends and other family members

Many potential suicides can be averted if the suicidal student talks about his or her problems with a good listener. Such discussions can take place in group counseling or may occur one-on-one. After helping the suicidal teen talk about their problems, the "good listener" can refer him or her to a professional counselor.

Some teens will discuss suicide only with other teens. Because of this tendency, teaching teenagers to help each other is a common strategy in schools around the country. Students are trained to listen to their classmates and to spot a student who may have a problem. Using their training, the peer counselors help troubled students confide in them and then refer the troubled students to professional counselors.

Don't ignore this problem in your classroom. Talking about suicide and the reasons for it really helps students considering suicide. Consider displaying the Where to Get Help poster on page 28 in your classroom. Most reasons young people give for killing themselves can be solved or will work themselves out in time. It's important to remind students that hard times usually are temporary. It is also important to get these students professional counseling as quickly as possible.

Remember, if a child confides in you that he or she is considering suicide, never keep it a secret. The student will probably be angry with you for "violating" his or her trust, but saving his or her life is more important than keeping a confidence. Telling someone shows that you care. Getting a potential suicide victim professional help is the best prevention.

WHAT WAS HIS NAME AGAIN?

Nancy Duffy Hery

Do some students feel invisible at school? Why do kids decide that some students don't deserve to be their friend? What can happen to a child who is constantly teased and left out of the group? Are there really students that even the teacher doesn't know their name?

Characters:

Stephanie	DuWayne	Summer
Shaleen	Travis	Emily
Jenna	Dion	Teacher
Cody	Caitlyn	Counselor
Alyssa	Jose	Chad Stevens

Scene 1   **It's early morning, and Stephanie, Shaleen, and Jenna are walking to school during a snowstorm. Cody is standing off to one side.**

Stephanie:
I can't wait to get to the ski lodge this afternoon.

Shaleen:
Me either. I've never been skiing before, and it looks like so much fun. Are you renting your equipment or are you bringing your own stuff?

Stephanie:
I didn't want to bother hauling everything with me, so I'm gonna rent.

Jenna:
Who cares about skiing anyway? I plan on sitting in the lodge most of the time lookin' at all the guys. I can't wait!

Shaleen:
You mean you're spending all that money to go on this trip and you don't want to ski?

Jenna:
Are you kidding me? I hate anything that requires sweating and messing up my hair. Don't you love the outfit I bought to wear?

Stephanie:
It sure doesn't look very warm.

From *Drama That Delivers*. © 1996. Teacher Ideas Press. (800) 237-6124.

Shaleen:
Don't you understand, Steph? She doesn't care.

Jenna:
Hey, isn't that Cody standing over there on Third Street?

Stephanie:
Yeah. Hey, Cody! What are you doing over here so early?

Cody joins the girls.

Cody:
Alyssa called me this morning and asked me to meet her here at 7:30. I've been standing here for half an hour and she's still not here.

Shaleen:
I wonder what's so important?

Jenna:
Yeah, she seemed fine when I talked to her last night. She was looking forward to the trip.

Cody:
Well, she sounded kind of upset, so I told her I'd meet her here and walk her to school.

Shaleen:
I don't know, but if we don't get going we're going to miss the tour bus. Besides, I'm freezing. Come on, let's meet her there.

Cody:
I guess you're right. Maybe she went by before I got here.

The group begins to exit. Alyssa runs up. She is breathless.

Alyssa:
Hey, Cody, wait up!

Cody:
It's about time.

Alyssa:
Listen, I'm sorry, but I had to cut through some yards and take the long way.

Shaleen:
Why'd you do that?

Alyssa:
Because someone is following me to school every day. That's why I called you, Cody. I don't know who it is.

Stephanie:
Did you tell your parents?

Alyssa:
Are you kidding? They are so protective that if I tell them I think someone is following me, they'll never let me go out alone again.

Jenna:
It's probably just your imagination. You know how dark mornings are in winter. Sometimes when the wind howls and the branches creak, it sounds like someone is behind you.

Alyssa:
I'm positive. When I stop and turn around the person dashes into the trees, or behind cars. I think it might be the same person who keeps leaving flowers and notes at my locker.

Cody:
Now I'm getting a little ticked.

Shaleen:
It's probably just some guy who has a crush on you.

Jenna:
Yeah, you're not the easiest person to talk to, either.

Stephanie:
Hey, everyone is already starting to load their stuff on the bus. Let's hustle.

Alyssa:
Let's try to figure this out when we get on the bus.

Scene 2   DuWayne, Travis, Dion, Caitlyn, Jose, Summer, Shaleen, Emily, Cody, and Stephanie are loading ski equipment onto the bus.

DuWayne:
I haven't gotten up this early in a long time. As soon as I get on the bus I'm going to sleep.

From *Drama That Delivers*. © 1996. Teacher Ideas Press. (800) 237-6124.

Travis:
Yeah, right, as if it will be quiet enough to sleep.

Dion:
Man, DuWayne can sleep through anything. Have you ever been over to his house with all those little brothers and sisters around? He sleeps through all that noise.

DuWayne:
You got that right! Hey, Caitlyn, grab me a seat by the window in the back!

Caitlyn:
OK, as long as you promise not to snore. I want to read a book on the way.

Caitlyn gets on the bus. One by one, the others follow her as they continue their conversation.

Jose:
I'm so glad it snowed last night. By the time we get to the hill, this fresh powder will be perfect.

Travis:
I'm going on the steepest run I can find.

DuWayne:
Yeah, right!

Summer:
Well, you'll be right over there with Mr. Nerd.

Jose:
Yeah, why'd he even come? I hope I don't get stuck in his cabin.

Shaleen:
Why are you picking on him? He doesn't say much, and he doesn't bother anyone.

Summer:
Have you seen how he dresses? And did you notice the outfit he had on today? It's embarrassing to be around him.

Emily:
Embarrassing! How'd you like to be me? He asked me on a date the other day in the hallway in front of everyone. I'll never live that down.

Dion:
Oh, yeah, like everyone can't wait to go out with you.

Emily:
Shut up, Dion. I don't see you running over to sit by him on the bus.

Dion:
I hardly know him.

Travis:
He's a dork. A real loser. He doesn't have any friends.

Caitlyn:
Where does he live?

Cody:
Who knows? No one really talks to him.

Chad gets off the bus and walks slowly to stage left.

Stephanie:
Quiet, he's getting off the bus to get something. I think he heard what everyone was saying.

Emily:
Those kind are always quiet.

Cody:
I heard someone locked him in the bathroom the other day and he couldn't get out.

Dion:
Get outta here.

As the conversation continues, Chad fumbles in his pocket, swallows something, then slowly sits down.

Cody:
Yeah, when they heard him yelling for help, he was in the bathroom crying. (*Cody laughs*)

Shaleen:
What's so funny about that?

The teacher enters.

Teacher: (*clapping her hands*)
Come on everybody, pick your seats. I want to make sure everyone is here.

Chad slowly lies down.

Stephanie:
Don't leave yet. One of the kids just got off the bus and went over towards the trees.

Teacher:
According to the roll sheet, everyone is here.

Jose:
Hey, look over by the trees. What is that lying in the snow?

Shaleen:
It looks like a person!

The teacher runs over to the trees. All the students follow her.

Cody:
It's that weird kid from the bus. Is he sick or something? He doesn't look like he's moving.

Dion:
Oh man, he has no pulse. Look at that prescription bottle next to him. What is it? I think he took all of them. Someone call 911!

Teacher:
The bus driver called on her radio. The ambulance is on the way. Everyone get out of the way.

Jose:
Who is it?

Caitlyn:
He was that kid who just got off the bus. He pretty much kept to himself.

Scene 3   The next day at school. The teacher and counselor are talking in the front office.

Counselor:
I can't believe what a tragedy this is. Did you read the note he left in his pocket?

Teacher:
Yeah, it was awful. He said he was tired of everyone making fun of him, and that he had no friends and wanted to die. He also said to tell Alyssa Peterson he was sorry for following her to school, but he was hoping if he saw her alone she wouldn't be embarrassed and might become his friend.

Counselor:
What was his name again?

Teacher:
Ya know, I can never remember.

Counselor:
It says here that his name was Chad Stevens and he was in your first period class. You don't remember him?

Teacher:
I guess he was just one of those invisible kids. Nothing really special about him.

Counselor:
His records show that he was a bright kid until the last couple of years. He was even in the gifted program, but dropped out of it. Then his grades started to slide. I'm surprised no one ever sent him to talk to me. The sad part is that there are so many other kids out there just like him, with the same kind of problems. I wish kids could understand they aren't alone no matter what their problems are.

Teacher:
I wonder what the other kids thought about him. What was his name again?

Counselor:
Chad. Chad Stevens.

Teacher:
Have you met with his parents yet?

Counselor:
I think he lives with his uncle. Apparently, the uncle has made the funeral arrangements. Someone will represent the school. We also have grief counselors here for the other students.

Teacher:
This is terrible.

Counselor:
We have grief counselors here for students—and teachers.

Scene 4   **All of the students, except Chad, gather in the school hallway the next morning.**

From *Drama That Delivers*. © 1996. Teacher Ideas Press. (800) 237-6124.

Jose:
Man, can you believe what everyone is saying about the kid who overdosed near the bus?

Cody:
Yeah, I hear he left a note saying that no one liked him.

Dion:
What a nut! Maybe if he wasn't so goofy he would have had more friends.

Shaleen:
Oh come on, Dion. Did you even know his name? Did you even give him a chance?

Dion:
Well, I don't hang out with that kind of kid.

Alyssa:
I feel badly, because he was the kid following me. He just wanted a chance to talk to me without my friends around.

Summer:
Now that I think about it, he did help me with my science project. I think he was even in my gifted class a few years ago.

Emily:
And whenever anyone needed lunch money, he was the first to give it to them.

DuWayne:
When someone stole my history book, he let me use his until I could get another one.

Travis:
What was his name again?

Caitlyn:
Chad. Chad Stevens. I guess he felt not being liked was enough reason to kill himself.

Alyssa:
We didn't even give him a chance. And now it's too late. We judged him without getting to know him.

Dion:
Well, there's nothing we can do about it now. Those kind of people do that all the time to themselves.

Cody:
What kind of people, Dion? You just said you didn't even know him.

Dion:
You know what I mean.

DuWayne:
Yeah, Dion, you're the one that was always picking on him in the halls.

Dion:
Oh sure, what about Emily? She embarrassed him in front of people anytime she could.

Emily:
Me? What about Jose and Summer? They were always teasing him.

Travis:
Listen to us. Trying to blame each other. There's nothing we can do now, except not let it happen again.

Shaleen:
I know I'm not going to judge people by first impressions ever again.

Jose:
Yeah, we all say that now, because we feel badly about it, but in about a week there will be another kid that everyone picks on.

Cody:
What do *we* do to stop this from happening again?

Alyssa:
I guess we shouldn't judge people by what they look like or how they dress.

Caitlyn:
Yeah. What was his name again?

WHERE TO GET HELP

Sometimes, it's easier to talk on the phone to a stranger than to talk to a person you know. If you find yourself wanting to talk to someone, or if you are depressed or in despair, try calling a teenage help hot line. Some hot lines are listed here. You can find others in the telephone directory. If you need to talk to someone right away and you don't know who to call, ask the operator to connect you to a hot line.

The following hot lines are good anywhere in the country—and they're free. You don't have to pay for the phone call. Remember, you don't have to give your name.

Suicide Intervention
24-Hour Hot Line
1 (800) 444-9999

Al-Anon and Alateen
1 (800) 356-9996

National Center for Exploited Children
1 (800) 843-5678

Adolescent Suicide
Hot Line
1 (800) 621-4000

WHERE TO GET HELP

QUESTIONS FOR DISCUSSION

1. Why are people so quick to label other people? (Example: a nerd or a dork)

2. Describe the type of character Chad Stevens was.

3. How did you feel when you read about Chad's suicide? Could it have been avoided?

4. What did you think about the teacher? Is it the teacher's responsibility to be aware of what is going on in the student's lives? Why?

5. What did you think about the students in this school? Are they typical? Why or why not?

6. What are some other ways that some young people make others outcasts?

RECOMMENDED READINGS

Fiction

Guest, Judith. *Ordinary People*. New York: Viking Press, 1976.

Peck, R. *Remembering the Good Times*. New York: Delacorte Press, 1985.

Nonfiction

Klagsbrun, Francine. *Too Young to Die: Suicide and Youth*. Boston: Houghton Mifflin, 1976.

McCoy, Kathleen. *Coping with Teenage Depression: A Parent's Guide*. New York: New American Library, 1982.

Roos, Stephen. *You'll Miss Me When I'm Gone*. New York: Delacorte Press, 1988.

IDEAS FOR ACTIVITIES

Suicide prevention activities are one part of a mental health unit. They deal with how to handle stress in a positive manner. The following enhancement activities involve dealing with stress as well as suicide prevention.

Speakers

Many speakers are available to talk to your class about mental health. Listings in your local telephone directory, under "Suicide" or "Mental health agencies," should provide numbers for organizations that may be willing to send a speaker to your classroom.

Creative Activity

After reading the play and answering the discussion questions, the students form groups and rewrite the play to include ways they could have helped Chad. This provides the opportunity to review and revise the plot.

Group Activity

Groups of five students list 10 stressful situations and 10 ways to handle these situations in a constructive manner. Students describe options for dealing with each situation and the consequences, both good and bad, of each option.

Language Arts

Each student writes a story in which the main character has a sad life or experiences a sad or tragic event but manages to come to terms with the experiences and emerges happier, wiser, or stronger at the end.

Class Activity

Discuss songs and movies that deal with suicide. What messages do they convey?

Group Activity

To help someone in a stressful situation, one needs to be a good friend and listener. In small groups, students list on a large piece of butcher paper 10 qualities of a good listener. After 10 minutes, the groups share their lists with the class.

Peer Counseling

Pairs of students are presented with a problem. One student pretends the problem is his or hers; the other practices being a good listener and tries to counsel the first student. The students then switch roles. If you have peer counselors at your school, have them come in to your classroom to demonstrate how this exercise is done.

REFERENCES

Gardner, Sandra, with Dr. Gary Rosenberg. *Teenage Suicide.* Englewood Cliffs, NJ: Silver Burdett Press and Simon & Schuster, 1985.

Kolehmainen, Janet. *Teen Suicide.* Minneapolis, MN: Lerner Publications, 1986.

McGuire, Leslie. *Suicide.* Vero Beach, FL: Rourke Corporation, 1990.

Miller, Michael. *Dare to Live.* Hillsboro, OR: Beyond Words Publishing, 1989.

3

The Ever-Changing Family

The current state of the family is a highly debated issue. Family demographics have been changing throughout this century. These changes may sometimes create difficulties, but they also make for a diverse society. Whether these changes are considered good or bad depends on how we learn to deal with them. Just what is a normal family? There isn't one single pattern but a potpourri of selections.

Families in the United States have undergone many changes since the 1800s. In the nineteenth century, one of the main reasons for having a large family was to have many children to work the fields or to help out financially. Also, families wanted to have a son to carry the family name. In the traditional nuclear family, the father's word was law; in the extended family, many relatives shared a home. Today's family has changed not only in size, but also in the roles family members now play.

Many factors affect the family system. Today more women work outside the home, families are smaller, and there are an increasing number of single-parent heads of households.

There are many types of families. In studying families we will talk about nuclear, single-parent, divorced, dysfunctional, adopted, foster, extended, homeless, and blended families. What do these terms mean?

1. Nuclear: Two parents, children

2. Single-parent: One parent, children

3. Blended: Two families joined together; step-family

4. Divorced: Parents divorced, share custody. For the sake of this discussion, divorced parents with sole custody are considered single-parent families

5. Extended: Additional family members, such as grandparents or cousins, live with the family

6. Dysfunctional: When family members do not fulfill their traditional roles

7. Foster: A temporary family for a child

8. Homeless: When the family has nowhere to live

One of the greatest changes in the American family has been the increase in single-parent homes. One out of every two marriages ends in divorce. Often with divorce comes new marriages and step-families. All of these people must learn to live with each other. There is no such thing anymore as the typical American family. Children must understand that not all families fit a certain image; it is all right to be different. The average family has disagreements, stresses, and problems. The important thing is to learn how to work them out. A real family is there to support, love, and respect each family member.

In a family of divorce, children have many questions. Is it difficult to live in a divorced family? What would it be like to have step-brothers and -sisters? Will I have to choose which parent I want to live with? Is it my fault that my parents are getting a divorce?

A divorce can create many problems for both the parents and the children. Are things as hopeless as they may seem? The following play will let your students see how one family handles the situation of the mother dating after her divorce from the father. When your class is finished, the students will have the opportunity to answer questions and discuss how they could handle this situation if it happens to them.

IT'S NOT MY FAULT YOU GOT A DIVORCE!

Nancy Duffy Hery

Everyone in a family is affected by divorce. Besides the problems stemming from the divorce itself, new involvements can make life very difficult. Are things as hopeless as they seem for everyone?

Characters:

Kathy Carter	Tina	Marco
John Carter	Maria	Eric Hoffman
Mom—Mrs. Carter	Jamie	Keith
Susan Carter	James Hoffman	Bob—Mr. Hoffman

Scene 1 **Kathy, Susan, and John are sitting in the living room with Mom discussing the day's events.**

Kathy:

I can't believe you're doing this to us. It's bad enough that you got rid of Dad, but now you want us to accept this new guy!

John:

Me, either. . . . I'm not going over to meet him and his stupid kids. Why can't you go alone?

Mom:

Please give Bob a chance. We've been dating for quite a while, and he wants you all to meet his children.

Kathy:

Why should we have to? You're the one going out with him, not us. I refuse to go. You can't make me.

John:

If you hadn't fought with Dad so much, this would never have happened. Why can't we be like other kids with a Mother and a Father?

Mom:

What do you mean? You have a Mother and a Father. We just live in separate houses. I know you don't understand why Dad and I broke up, but we just didn't get along with each other anymore. Isn't it better to be apart than to have us screaming at each other all of the time?

John:

No, I hate this Bob guy. I hate all the guys you go out with. I would rather have Dad back, screaming and all.

Susan:

I hope he doesn't have kids that he plans to bring with him. I am not giving up my room for anyone.

Mom:

I am sorry that your Father and I divorced, but it happened and we must go on with our lives.

Susan:

Sure, go on with your life, Mom. Don't even consider our feelings.

Mom:

I am considering your feelings, and I think that all of you are being very selfish. You won't even give this a chance. How do you know that you won't like Bob and his children?

John:

I am sick of this big guilt trip you are trying to lay on us. We are not the ones who got the divorce. We are not the ones who want to get along with this guy and his kids. It's you, Mom, and we don't care. We got along fine without this guy and his kids.

Mom:

Well, I'll tell you what. . . . I am not going to give you an option on this. I tried to be nice and patient, but I think that all of you are being pretty childish. Now, I am going to tell it to you straight. We are going over to Bob's house today and you are going to be polite. I really can't believe how rudely you are treating me. I am sick of it. Now get dressed and get ready. I don't want to hear another word from any of you. Understand?

All kids:

Yes, Mom.

Scene 2 **Tina, Maria, and Jamie stop at the house to talk to the girls. Tina, Maria, Jamie, Susan, and Kathy are standing on the front porch.**

Tina:

Hey, Susan, do you and Kathy want to go to the movies with us this afternoon?

Susan:

I wish we could. My Mom has this serious boyfriend that she wants us to meet.

Kathy: (*sarcastic*)
Yeah, what a fun time that should be.

Maria:
It might not be too bad. My Mom just remarried, and I really like Allan a lot. He's a lot nicer than my Dad. He doesn't try to replace my Dad, just be a friend to my brothers and I.

Jamie:
I hate when my Mom dates guys, too. The biggest problem around my house is the child support checks. If my Dad owes us money, Mom makes me call and try to get it from him.

Tina:
You have to call your Dad and ask for money?

Jamie:
Yeah, if we want to pay rent and eat that month.

Tina:
Man, I better go home and hug my parents tonight.

Jamie:
Oh, it's not as bad as it sounds. I just hate when my parents put me in the middle of them.

Maria:
I used to hate when my Dad always wanted to know what my Mom's dates were like. He always asked me so many questions. He's stopped doing that now that he has remarried.

Susan:
I guess we should stop complaining and go out with my Mom tonight. It sounds like you guys had some of the same problems.

Kathy:
You can be polite, but I'm not. Just watch how she'll act around his children. She'll be all mushy and polite to them.

Maria:
Well, I guess you can't go to the show.

Susan:
You'll have to go without us. Call us tonight when you get home.

Scene 3   Bob's house. James, Marco, Eric, and Keith are sitting on the patio, talking.

James:
If I had known that my Dad was bringing over some girlfriend of his and her kids I wouldn't have come over this weekend.

Marco:
Yeah, my Dad does the same thing to me. It's supposed to be the weekend with me and he always ends up bringing some stupid woman along. I hate it so much I don't even go over to his house as much as I used to.

James:
After my parents split, I always hoped they'd get back together. They seemed real friendly with each other, and there weren't any money problems. I guess that's why I resent this new jerk.

Marco:
Have you ever had to meet any of your Dad's girlfriends before?

Eric:
Yeah, but they were nothing serious. We just blew them off and played the game.

James:
Do you ever wish when you see your parents together that they might get back together?

Keith:
All the time. Can you believe it? Even though they used to scream at each other. . . . I guess I'm kinda weird.

Marco:
Not really, I do the same thing.

James:
Yeah, but you guys still haven't helped us figure a way out of meeting this family today.

Keith:
Hey, tell your Dad you already have plans with your Mom. That always works: Play one against the other.

Eric:
No, I don't want to do that. Then my Dad would be calling my Mom and it would be a mess. Maybe we could just be mean to this lady's kids.

Marco:
Does she have any daughters?

James:
Yeah, two of them. They're probably dogs.

Bob comes out on the patio.

Bob:
Hey, guys. We're going to be cooking out here on the grill this afternoon. It looks like your friends will have to leave now so we can get cleaned up.

Eric:
Geez, what for?

James:
I'm not changing clothes. I look fine.

Keith:
Hey, we gotta go. Remember what I told you.

Bob:
What was that all about?

James:
Nothing. I'm not feeling very well. I think I'm gonna call Mom and see if she can come get me.

Bob:
Are you feeling hot? Maybe you should lie down for awhile.

Eric:
Yeah, we're sick, Dad. We're sick of the thought of meeting your newest girlfriend. Why don't you leave us out of this?

Bob:
Why don't you two grow up and give me a break? Now go inside and get ready. They'll be here in about half an hour.

Scene 4   **Upstairs in the bedroom at the Jackson residence. Kathy, Susan, and John are hanging around—*not* getting ready to go.**

Kathy:

Boy, Mom sure got excited. We may have to go, but I am not going to be nice. I'll put on my fakey smile for those brats, but as soon as the adults leave I'll let 'em have it.

Susan:

Maybe we should give them a chance. Mom really likes this guy, and I think she wants to marry him.

Kathy:

Can you imagine if she does marry him? We'd have to move from our neighborhood and lose all our friends.

John:

If she marries this guy, I'm out of here. I don't care where I have to live. Maybe Dad will let me live with him. The only bad part about living with Dad is that now he has kids at the other house, too. I hate this family. I wish I could divorce this set of parents myself.

Susan:

You don't mean that. You love Mom and Dad.

Kathy:

I hate this family, too. Why should we have to go through this? Dad moves out, gets married again, has another family, and now we are like the step-children. I always feel like I don't belong when we go to his house. It's like we are visitors.

Susan:

I don't think we are visitors to Dad. He always buys us stuff and takes us places.

John:

Someone please shut her up. Gimme a break. Dad is just too busy for us.

Kathy:

Quiet, John. Dad is not the problem right now.

Susan:

Here comes Mom.

Mom enters the bedroom and the kids are quiet.

Mom:

Please try to be nice. I know you don't understand what I am going through, but I just want a shot at happiness. Don't you guys see how nice Bob is to me? Don't you remember how Dad and I used to fight all the time? It wasn't pleasant around here. Your Dad and I still love all of you equally, but we just aren't married to each other anymore. You know it was for the best. Don't you want me to be happy, too?

Susan:

Mom, we want you to be happy. Why do you need another man to be happy? What's wrong with just us? Don't we make you happy enough?

Mom:

Of course you make me happy. But I need adult companionship, too. And where will I be when you move out on your own? Why won't you give this man a chance?

Susan:

Mom, don't start crying.

John:

Mom, I'm sorry, but I hate this. I can't be fakey, and I don't want to go. Let me stay home.

Kathy:

I don't want to go, either.

Mom:

Well, thanks a lot. I feel like everyone is against me. First your Father and now you.

John:

Oh man, don't start laying that guilt trip on us.

Mom:

Well, I am tired of playing games with everyone. You are all going and you are going to be pleasant. I'll see you downstairs in five minutes.

From *Drama That Delivers.* © 1996. Teacher Ideas Press. (800) 237-6124.

QUESTIONS FOR DISCUSSION

1. How would you feel if you were the Carter children? How would you have handled this situation?

2. Do you think parents sometimes act this way? How would you describe their behavior?

3. Do you think the children were being selfish? Were they realistic?

4. Do divorced parents ever put their children in the middle? What does that do to the children?

5. Do the Carter and Hoffman kids have anything in common? Do you think they can become friends—or at least get along?

6. What do you think happened when both families got together?

7. Do kids sometimes blame themselves for their parents' problems? Why do they do this?

RECOMMENDED READINGS

Fiction

Bunting, Anne. *A Part of the Dream.* New York: Fearon, 1978.

Danzinger, Paula. *It's an Aardvark Eat Turtle World.* New York: Dell, 1985.

Fox, Paula. *Moonlight Man.* New York: Broadway Press, 1986.

Kropp, Paul. *Dirt Bike.* New York: EMC, 1982.

Mazer, Harry. *Guy Lenny.* New York: Dell, 1979.

Paulsen, Gary. *Hatchet.* New York: Puffin Books, 1987.

Spinelli, Jerry. *Maniac Magee.* New York: Little, Brown, 1990.

Nonfiction

Gardner, Richard A. *Boys and Girls Book About Divorce.* New York: Bantam Books, 1970.

Garigan, Elizabeth. *Living with Divorce.* New York: Good Apple, 1991.

Johnson, Linda Carlson. *Everything You Need to Know About Your Parents' Divorce.* New York: Rosen, 1989.

Krementz, Jill. *How It Feels When Parents Divorce.* New York: Alfred A. Knopf, 1988.

LeShan, Eda J. *What's Going to Happen to Me?* New York: Aladdin, 1978.

IDEAS FOR ACTIVITIES

Language Arts

Students think of five different television families and answer the following questions: How are these television families like yours? How do they handle problems? Are they realistic? Compare and contrast television families of yesterday to television families of today.

Geography and History

Students investigate the customs of families around the world. Interview family members to find out customs of their family and find out where their family is from. This is also a good time to have a cultural awareness fair with different types of foods from different cultures and families.

Science and Health

Students investigate their family trees. With the teacher supplying information as needed, the class discusses genetic characteristics, including which characteristics are recessive and which are dominant. After students create their family trees, discuss the health aspects of genetic traits. In particular, explain which disorders, such as sickle-cell anemia, Tay-Sachs disease, or Down's syndrome, are genetic.

Technology

Students role play a family counselor. Distribute a slip of paper naming a family problem to each student. The students offer counseling to the whole family by typing their responses on the computer. Using the computer is fun and alleviates students' fears that others will identify their writing.

Creative Activity

In groups of five, students devise an ending to the play. Students may perform their ending for the class.

Community Service

Students volunteer to help out homeless or needy families in the area. Sometimes direct involvement is the best way to learn about how other families live.

Speakers

Speakers can be found to discuss family issues through a number of organizations, including United Way agencies. Also counseling and other family-oriented organizations usually enjoy sharing with students.

Station Teaching

Students form groups of six, and each group goes to one of six stations. The groups brainstorm responses to that station's questions or activities, then rotate to the next station. They work as a team and only have seven minutes at each station. After the groups get through all the stations, they will share their responses with the class, if there is time.

- List 10 qualities of good parents.
- List five qualities of bad parents.
- Write down 10 household chores. When finished, figure out which chores should be done by children, which ones by parents.
- Write three different classified advertisements for parents, as if they would be published in the newspaper.
- Present two hypothetical family situations; the group decides what to do as a family.
- Make up a recipe describing a family and a recipe describing parents.

Art and Design

Check the library for books about family crests. After sharing these with your students, the students design their own family crests. Students can also make a collage of pictures of their family.

Physical Education

Through the physical education department, students plan a family night of activities. Students design fun games that can involve everyone. This family night is also a good time to display students' collages and invented family crests around the room.

REFERENCES

Glassman, Bruce. *Everything You Need to Know About Step Families.* New York: Rosen, 1988.

Powledge, Fred. *You'll Survive!* New York: Charles Scribner's Sons, 1986.

Raab, Robert A. *Coping with Divorce.* New York: Rosen, 1979.

Sheehy, Gail. *Passages.* New York: E. P. Dutton, 1976.

4

Eating Disorders

An eating disorder is an affliction of extreme and damaging eating behaviors that can lead to sickness and even death. Because eating sensibly seems so simple, it is hard to imagine that this illness is increasing rapidly in the United States. However, eating sensibly may sound easy to you, but to someone with an eating disorder it is a daily, hated ritual.

Why won't some people eat? Why would anyone try to vomit constantly? Why are girls starving to death? This problem is more common than people imagine.

There are three types of eating disorders. The first one, called anorexia nervosa, is a severe fear of becoming overweight that often leads to self-starvation.

Still, you might ask, why do people with this disorder keep losing weight once they are thin? Anorexic people still feel fat no matter what weight they obtain. When they look in a mirror, they still see a very fat person.

Teenagers may be insecure about their physical appearance. They may feel that in order to be perfect in our culture they must be extremely thin. Sometimes girls and boys involved in activities that focus on weight control become obsessed with it. Every case is different.

The following are some of the warning signs of anorexia nervosa:

- Excessive exercise in spite of fatigue
- Extreme fear of weight gain
- Not eating, just playing with food at the table
- Abnormal weight loss with no known cause
- Constant discussion about food or weight loss
- Changes in personality
- Large reduction of food intake
- Problems with skin and menstruation

The second eating disorder is called bulimia. Bulimia is a condition in which people binge (uncontrollable overeating), then purge (vomit or use laxatives). This binging and purging is usually done in secret, because people with this disorder are embarrassed by their behavior. The difference between bulimics and anorexics is that bulimics will turn to food when they are depressed, while anorexics turn away from it. Bulimics are also harder to identify.

The following are some of the warning signs of bulimia:

- Any evidence of a binge-purge cycle

- Concern for secrecy

- Concern about weight and attempts to control it through dieting, vomiting, and laxatives

- Constant depression about weight

- Large quantities of food consumed in secret

The third eating disorder is obesity. Many young people become extremely overweight because of emotional problems. Food becomes a friend to them, and they feel it can heal whatever pain they feel. When children overeat and become extremely heavy, they need not only physical help but emotional help as well. A diet alone will not help them lose weight and keep it off. They must first learn why they are overeating.

How can we help them? What can you do if one or more of your students has an eating disorder? First of all, they cannot cure themselves. They do not have a realistic view of themselves. The best thing that you can do is refer them to a counselor. If the illness is too severe, the student may need to be hospitalized. Don't keep it a secret. You may save someone's life by revealing his or her problem.

In the following drama, one of the girls is starving herself. Her friends feel that she has a problem, but no one wants to tell her parents or teachers about it. The starvation diet and overexercise have developed to the point that her teachers and friends must step in and help her.

YOU CAN NEVER BE TOO THIN

Nancy Duffy Hery

The health risks of poor nutrition, anorexia, and bulimia are a serious problem with our youth.

Characters:

Jason	Tony	Stacey
Luke	Alecia	Ms. Johnson
Brandy	Reggie	Mr. Hernandez
Jill		

Scene 1   **Jason, Luke, Brandy, Jill, Tony, Alecia, and Reggie are walking in from physical education class.**

Jason:
Where's Stacey?

Luke:
She's still out on the track.

Brandy:
Man, when PE time is done, I run to get in here.

Jill:
Me too! If you ask me, she's becoming obsessed with exercise.

Tony:
You girls are just jealous because she's in such great shape.

Alecia:
We are not jealous. We are just not crazy enough to keep running in this heat.

Luke:
While you all talk, I'm going to hit the showers. Talk to Stacey later and see if maybe she got into trouble with the coach.

Brandy:
I'll tell you what, she's really losing the weight. She told me she has already lost 14 pounds, and she wasn't fat before. I wish I could lose some weight.

Tony:
Please, where would you lose it? The only place fat on you is your fat head!

Luke:
I get sick of girls asking me all the time, "Am I too fat?"

Jason:
Me, too. It's like they are fishing for a compliment. They always pretend like they don't want to eat anything and that they eat like birds. How stupid can you get?

Reggie:
I like girls to have a little meat on them, anyway. I can't stand hugging a girl who feels like her bones are going to shatter.

Jill:
As if any girls would want to hug you anyway.

Luke:
Yeah, the only girl he's hugging is his Mommy.

Reggie:
Shut up, Thin Man. At least I have a great bod to hug.

Brandy:
Please, don't make us gag.

Alecia:
No one understands what I'm saying about Stacey.

Tony:
So, what's your point?

Jill:
Do you think she has that eating disorder that Mr. Hernandez was talking about in class the other day?

Luke:
Oh come on, not Stacey. She's really smart, cute, and does really well in all her classes. She's a real competitor.

Alecia:
That's what I mean. She's got a lot of the characteristics of an anorexic. They want to be in control of everything, be the best at everything, and that includes their weight.

Jill:
Yeah, but I don't think she would starve herself.

Reggie:
Here she comes now. Why don't you ask her how she's losing all the weight and why?

Brandy:
Let's wait until we're in the locker room.

Jason:
Hey, Stacey, are you trying to get in good with the coach or something?

Stacey:
No, I'm just trying to lose a couple extra pounds before track season.

Brandy:
You look fine, Stacey.

Stacey:
Everybody says that, but as the saying goes, "You can never be too rich or too thin."

Brandy:
You can't believe those stupid lines or try to look like the models. They all starve themselves to look like that.

Stacey:
Yeah, you say that, but isn't it true that all guys want their girlfriends to look like models?

Reggie:
They're just playin' with you. We don't want you to look like a bone rack, either. If you're too thin, you won't have the energy to run track, either.

Stacey:
Remember that when I'm slim and trim and hard to beat. Quit nagging me, I've got to take a shower.

Scene 2   In the girls' locker room. Brandy, Stacey, and Jill are packing their gym bags.

Brandy:
You look like you've lost more weight, Stacey.

Stacey:
Isn't it great? I'm dieting and running, and the best part is that it's so easy. I still can't lose all the weight I need to lose, though.

Jill:
You're thin enough. You don't need to lose any more. You're getting too thin. You're starting to scare us.

Stacey:
As far as I'm concerned, I can never be too thin.

Brandy:
Hey, we're late for class. Let's go.

Stacey:
You girls go ahead. I'll get a pass from Ms. Johnson.

Brandy and Jill exit. Stacey goes into a bathroom stall and begins to vomit. Ms. Johnson comes into the locker room. She hears Stacey vomiting and thinks that she is very ill.

Ms. Johnson:
Are you OK?

Stacey:
Yeah, I'm better now, Ms. Johnson. I must have run too much on the track and it made me a little sick.

Ms. Johnson:
Do you want to call home? Maybe you should lie down for awhile.

Stacey:
No, really.

Ms. Johnson:
I'll wait here for you and write you a pass.

Stacey:
I'll be right there.

Ms. Johnson:
Stacey, have you been ill for the past month? I'm worried about how thin you're getting.

Stacey:
No, I just have a high metabolism and I haven't been that hungry lately.

Ms. Johnson:
You need to eat in order to play any athletics this year.

Stacey:
I'll be in the best shape yet.

Ms. Johnson:
If you have anymore problems today, feel free to come see me, and we'll call your Mom.

Stacey:
Thanks, Ms. Johnson. Listen, I gotta go.

Scene 3   Classroom scene with teacher discussion. Mr. Hernandez is leading a discussion among Reggie, Luke, Brandy, Jill, Tony, Alecia, and Jason.

Mr. Hernandez:
Anorexia nervosa is an eating disorder that is a severe fear of becoming overweight. It often leads to extreme weight loss from self-starvation.

Reggie:
Can you catch it, like a cold or something?

Mr. Hernandez:
No, Reggie, it's a disorder of both the mind and the body. People with it are so afraid of becoming fat that they quit eating, make themselves vomit, or take diuretics or laxatives.

Luke:
Why would people do that to themselves? There is no way that I could stop eating.

Brandy:
It's mainly girls who do this, isn't it, Mr. Hernandez?

Mr. Hernandez:
Yes, Brandy, about 97 percent of the cases are girls. Why do you suppose that's so?

Jill:
That's easy to answer. All you have to do is watch TV, or pick up a magazine. All the girls are thin. Guys want their girlfriends to be thin.

Mr. Hernandez:
Do you think that's true, guys? Do we put pressure on girls to be thin?

Reggie:
I don't think guys put pressure on girls to be thin. They put it on themselves. We don't make them starve themselves.

Tony:
Yeah, girls who vomit up their food are sick.

Mr. Hernandez:
That's right. They are sick, Tony. They are emotionally and mentally ill. They feel that if they can control this aspect of their body, they can control anything. Usually they are the high achievers in the class—quiet girls who get along with everyone.

Luke:
Yeah, but about pressuring girls to be thin. Tell the truth, guys. Honestly, would you go out with a fat girl?

Alecia:
None of them are going to answer that, because they don't want us to nail them.

Brandy:
Yeah, our society constantly puts pressure on girls to be skinny.

Mr. Hernandez:
So, what's the solution to this problem?

Jason:
I don't think there's an easy solution, but we can help by letting girls know that we think having muscle tone is OK and your weight means nothing, if you try to stay in shape.

Alecia:
I constantly worry about my weight.

Reggie:
So, what do you weigh?

Alecia:
It's none of your business.

Jill:
Mr. Hernandez, what would you do if you had a friend who you think had this problem?

Mr. Hernandez:
Get her help as soon as possible. People don't realize the severity of this illness. She could die.

Stacey enters the classroom. She is late and gives the pass to Mr. Hernandez.

Stacey:
Sorry I'm late. I went to the office to call home. I'm not feeling well and will be leaving right now, Mr. Hernandez.

Mr. Hernandez:
OK, Stacey. Hope you are feeling better tomorrow.

Bell rings and class dismisses.

Scene 4   Stacey is at home sick. She receives a phone call from Brandy and Alecia.

Stacey:
Hello.

Alecia:
Hey, Stacey. I'm on a three-way call here with you and Brandy. We were worried about you today. You looked so pale.

Brandy:
You didn't faint or anything, did you?

Stacey:
When I went to the office to call my Mom, I felt pretty faint, so I came home. I feel better now.

Alecia:
Hey, Stacey, we're good friends right?

Stacey:
Yeah, why?

Alecia:
Brandy and I think you might be anorexic.

Stacey:
What are you talking about?

Brandy:
We think you may have an eating disorder.

Stacey:
You have got to be kidding. You know what your problem is? You know what everyone's problem is at that dumb school? They are all jealous. They are afraid that I will be slim and steal away their boyfriends. I'm glad I am not fat like both of you.

Alecia:
We think you're getting too thin. Maybe you should talk to someone.

Brandy:
Does your Mom know what you're doing?

Stacey:
What are you talking about? I eat all the time.

Alecia:
We both realized how pale you look, and your skin is starting to break out, too. Those are all signs of anorexia. I bet you no longer have your menstrual cycle, either.

Stacey:
That is none of your business. You two are just ganging up on me. I don't think we're friends anymore. (*slams down phone*)

Alecia:
We need to tell her Mom that we think she is sick.

Brandy:
She'll really hate us if we do.

Alecia:
I don't care. She is sick and needs our help. She doesn't realize how bad it is.

Brandy:
Let's go talk to her Mom at work.

Alecia:
We've got to do something.

QUESTIONS FOR DISCUSSION

1. How can you help a friend you think might have an eating disorder?

2. What are some warning signs of anorexia or bulimia?

3. What else can happen to your body if you stop eating or continue to vomit and gorge yourself?

4. Why do you think this disorder afflicts mainly girls aged 12 to 17?

5. What can we do as a society to fight this illness?

6. Do you think the students in the play handled this problem correctly? Please explain your answer.

7. Try to think of three TV commercials with women in them. Name them and tell if the girls are extremely slim.

RECOMMENDED READINGS

Nonfiction

Erlanger, Ellen. *Eating Disorders: A Question and Answer Book About Anorexia Nervosa and Bulimia.* Minneapolis, MN: Lerner Publications, 1988.

Kolodny, Nancy J. *When Food's a Foe: How to Confront and Conquer Eating Disorders.* New York: Little, Brown, 1987.

Sanchez, Gail Jones, and Mary Gerbino. *Overeating: Let's Talk About It.* Minneapolis, MN: Dillon Press, 1986.

IDEAS FOR ACTIVITIES

Class Activity

Students gather different types of diet plans, compile them, and write down the pros and cons of each diet.

Speakers

Speakers from local wellness centers will talk to students about exercise, diet, and proper nutrition. Sometimes the center will send a dietitian or counselor to talk with the students.

Media

Students gather from magazines many advertisements that feature girls and boys their age. They try to find an advertisement containing a picture of a girl or boy who looks healthy and not extremely thin, as well as an ad with a healthy person. Discuss the following questions: What do these ads portray? What are they trying to sell?

Life Skills

Students write down what they eat for three days. Along with this record they keep track of their exercise. They then compute the nutritional values and calories of their diet and the calories they expend in exercise to see if they are on the right track. Are they getting enough exercise and nutrition daily?

Math

Using an exercise chart that shows the number of calories burned through each exercise, students compute what they burned in one day.

Discussion

Eating disorders are sometimes caused by stress, social pressure, and trying to be thin. Discuss these causes in class and what can be done about them. Come up with a plan to prevent these factors from leading to an eating disorder.

Understanding

In a paragraph, students write the many health risks of starving themselves.

REFERENCES

Erlanger, Ellen. *Eating Disorders.* Minneapolis, MN: Lerner Publications, 1985.

Landau, Elaine. *Why Are They Starving Themselves?* New York: Messner, 1983.

Maloney, Michael and Rachel Kranz. *Straight Talk About Eating Disorders.* New York: Facts on File, 1991.

Woodward, Kathy. *Coping with a Negative Body Image.* New York: Rosen, 1989.

5

Peer Pressure: It's Your Choice

Many books and articles have been written in the past 20 years about peer pressure and problem solving. Problem solving involves choosing an option from many available choices. This skill entails specific steps that can be taught and practiced in the classroom. Problem solving is difficult for adolescents. The problems that they face can seem overwhelming to them. If they practice this skill, it will become easier for them to use it in difficult situations. The following steps will help students learn to work out their problems and predict the consequences of their actions.

1. Clearly identify the real problem. Know the basis of your problem.

2. Identify your options. Identify as many as you can.

3. Evaluate the consequences of each choice.

4. Select the best choice and act on it.

5. Evaluate the results. Was the problem solved? Could you have done a better job?

Of course, students won't use this process every time they have a problem. Practice it with them on small problems first, so that it becomes second nature to them. When a difficult problem arises, they will be prepared. Also, explain to your students that everyone make mistakes. It's OK to make mistakes. Students learn from their mistakes.

Many young people do not want to take responsibility for their actions. Many want to blame others or come up with excuses when things don't go smoothly for them. Becoming responsible is the key to becoming an adult.

Another way to improve decision making is through goal setting. When students have a goal, it gives them something to work toward. The following are some ideas to give to students about goal setting:

1. Choose one thing you want to work on.

2. List what you will do to reach your goal.

3. Set a specific period of time to accomplish your goal.

4. Set a reward for yourself.

The following play deals with students that have to make many decisions on their own. Do they make responsible choices? Are they ready to accept the consequences of their choices? How will they handle peer pressure? This play will help students cope successfully with their peers and society.

COME ON, ONE WON'T HURT!

Nancy Duffy Hery

Sometimes the best kids can fold under the pressure of their friends. These pressures can involve anything from skipping class, to drinking alcohol, or even cheating on an exam. All of these are different pressures, but the skills involved in making the right choice are the same. In this play, several students give in to peer pressure, but one does not.

Characters:

Matt	Rebecca	John
Charles	Bonnie	Colleen
David	Kevin	Tiffany
Jenna	Mary	7-11 store clerk
Janelle	Jeff	

Scene 1   All of the students are in the band room at school.

Matt:
How long are we supposed to be in the practice room today?

Charles:
Oh, Mr. Lopez got us out of class for two periods to practice for the concert.

David:
You know, he never comes down to check on us. I am sick of practicing. I've got my brother's car today, so lets book out of here and go over to my house for awhile.

Jenna:
Hey, he'll never even know we left. Let's go over to my house. My parents will be gone until Sunday.

Janelle:
Are you nuts? There is no way that I'm skipping out of practice to go to your house.

Rebecca:
Oh yeah, Miss Suck-Up herself. Geez, don't you ever want to have any fun? Mr. Lopez won't even miss us. It's not like we do this kind of thing every day.

Bonnie:
Hey, I wanna go. I've got my car here, too. We could stop at 7-11 first and get some food.

Kevin:
Man, I have never skipped before. My parents would kill me.

David:
That's your whole problem, Kevin. You're afraid of your own shadow. What your parents don't know won't kill them.

Mary:
If we go now, we can be back by fourth period. No one will miss us.

Jeff:
I'm not going. You guys go ahead. I'll stay in the practice room and cover for you if anyone comes around.

Charles:
Oh come on, Jeff. It's the end of the school year. What's one day's difference going to make? Don't be such a wimp. No wonder everyone thinks you're such a nerd.

Jeff:
Just because I don't want to skip doesn't make me a nerd.

John:
Yeah, right. Do you ever do anything wrong?

Janelle:
Lay off him, John. If he doesn't want to go, I understand. Listen, Jeff, I guess I'll go if you go.

John:
Oh, come on, Janelle.

Janelle hesitates, thinking.

Janelle:
Actually, it's kinda legal. We already have permission to be out of class, so we won't really get into trouble. Let's go.

Colleen:
All right, Janelle! She's actually going to do something fun for a change.

Bonnie:
Let's go before we change our minds. We'll go when the bell rings and stagger ourselves as we go to the cars. Everyone trusts us, so if we get stopped we'll just say we're going to pick up instruments that were being replaced.

Jeff:
I'll see you guys later. Have fun, Janelle.

Rebecca:
See ya, Jeff. (*whispers loudly*) Sometimes he acts like such a loser, doesn't he?

Tiffany:
I know. All he cares about is getting good grades and a band scholarship to college. He never wants to have any fun.

David:
Let's get going.

Scene 2   The students are in two cars, driving to Jenna's house. John, Matt, David, Mary, Kevin, and Rebecca are in one car. Jenna, Bonnie, Tiffany, Janelle, Charles, and Colleen are in the other car. David pulls into a 7-11 store parking lot.

John:
Hey, David, why are you stopping here?

Matt:
Hey, let me come with you. I have to go to the bathroom.

David:
Hey, Mary, would you come in, too? I need your help for a minute.

Mary:
Sure, no problem.

Scene 3   In the 7-11 store. Matt exits to the bathroom. David and Mary head to the back of the store. A clerk stands at the counter.

Mary:
David, what are you doing?

David:
Just give me your backpack and go up to the counter and buy some gum. Flirt with the guy, if you have to, to keep his attention.

Mary:
What?

David:
You heard what I said. Now we've been going out for four months, you know I love you, so just do this for me.

Mary:
OK.

Mary goes to the counter and flirts with the clerk. David stuffs things into the backpack. Matt returns from the bathroom, joining David.

David:
Hey, Matt, could you take Mary's backpack out for her? I need to get some other stuff.

Matt:
Sure. Man, is this thing heavy.

David:
Shut up and just take it out of here. Hey, Mary, hurry up and meet us in the car.

Mary:
I'll be right there.

They exit, Mary and Matt first. David stops to stuff something into his own backpack, then follows Mary out of the store.

Scene 4   Everyone is back in the car.

David:
Let's *party*!

Kevin:
How far is it to Jenna's house?

Rebecca:
About four blocks.

Janelle:
I still feel guilty about this. What if my parents find out?

Kevin:
Will you stop saying that? We'll be back in school before you know it. Let's enjoy this while we can.

Scene 5   At Jenna's house. All of the students—except Jeff—assemble.

Jenna:
Hey, David, I saw you guys run into the store. I hope you got something good to eat.

David:
Better than that, we got us some beer. I got two 12-packs into different backpacks.

Bonnie:
Are you serious? Open 'em up!

Jenna:
Just don't spill on my parents' carpet.

Charles:
How did you get the beer, anyway?

Matt:
No wonder the backpack was so heavy.

Janelle:
I can't believe I'm hearing this. First, you get me to skip class, and now you brought beer. Can someone take me back to school?

Kevin:
No one forced you to come here. Why don't you go in the other room and watch TV until it's time to go?

Janelle exits, shaking her head.

Janelle:
I can't believe you guys talked me into this.

Mary:
I'm glad she went into the back room. She's starting to get on my nerves. Now we can have some real fun.

John:
Hey, does anyone have a cigarette?

Tiffany:
Here, have one of mine.

Matt:
I didn't know you guys smoked.

John:
There's a lot of things you don't know about us.

David:
Hey, Mary, throw me another beer, will you?

Tiffany:
Let's go swimming!

Jenna:
I don't think my parents would like that. We're not allowed to swim when no one is home.

Kevin:
What they don't know won't kill them.

Charles:
I think that the first person that wants to go swimming is Rebecca.

Charles playfully grabs Rebecca and starts dragging her.

Rebecca:
Charles, get away from me! Charles, you better not! Help me Jenna, grab my arm!

Scene 6   At the pool at Jenna's house. Suddenly everyone is pushing everyone into the pool.

Bonnie:
Oh my gosh, how are we going to dry off before we go back to class?

David:
Everyone strip down to their underwear and let Jenna put the clothes in the dryer.

Mary:
Let's do it.

Rebecca:
Yeah, underwear are just like swimsuits, anyway. Stop it Matt. I can take my own clothes off.

Matt:
I'm just trying to help you get them off quicker.

Janelle:
What are you guys doing in the pool?

From *Drama That Delivers*. © 1996. Teacher Ideas Press. (800) 237-6124.

David:
What does it look like?

Janelle:
Put me down, Kevin! I mean it! Put me down or I'll kick you so hard you'll pass out.

John:
Throw her in, Kevin. Come on, let's help him.

Janelle:
Stop! Tiffany, make them stop!

Charles:
One, two, three . . . (*splash*)

Mary:
Hey, Janelle, quit playing around and come on out.

Bonnie:
What's all the red stuff coming up from the bottom?

Matt:
Oh my God, look at the blood on the edge of the pool. She must have hit her head when we threw her in.

Jenna:
Quick, dive down and get her. She's probably unconscious.

David dives in.

Tiffany:
I think David's got her now. Careful, she might have broken her back or something.

Bonnie:
Oh man, she's got a big gash on her head. Shouldn't we call 911 or something?

Jenna:
Geez, we are in deep trouble now. Charles, get rid of all the beer cans, I'll call 911.

Bonnie:
Is she breathing?

Colleen:
We are in trouble now. Quick, try to get the bleeding stopped. Is she breathing yet?

Rebecca:
I can't tell.

Charles:
Somebody do something before the ambulance gets here.

Tiffany:
How are we going to explain this to our parents?

Kevin:
It's your fault, Tiffany. You're the one who wanted to skip class and come here in the first place.

Tiffany:
I am not! David was.

Mary:
Everyone quit arguing and get rid of all the beer cans. It's bad enough that Janelle is hurt. We don't want the cops to see that we were drinking, too.

Colleen:
I can't believe this is happening to me. My parents are going to kill me.

David:
Shut up, Colleen. Listen—the police are on their way. Let's get our story straight before they get here. We were playing around and she fell in. We weren't skipping, we just came over here and we were going back.

John:
Oh yeah, like they'd believe that story.

David:
You got a better one?

Tiffany:
Let's tell them that, but leave out the part about drinking. If we get caught we could be suspended for 10 days.

Kevin:
I don't know about you guys, but I'm leaving right now out the back door. I'm not taking the fall with all of you. Let's go.

Colleen:

Me too. Come on, let's leave. That way only a few of us get into trouble, and it doesn't really look like a party, just a few kids coming home for lunch.

Mary:

I will never be able to go out for the rest of the year. My parents will never trust me again. I'm not leaving Janelle here to face the police alone.

Charles:

Quit your whining. Someone's at the door. Everyone sit still and act calm.

Bonnie:

Yeah right, act calm. All my work towards a scholarship is down the drain.

Matt:

I can't get Janelle's head to stop bleeding. She's going to need stitches, I think. She still seems unconscious, but she's breathing. I hope she's going to be OK.

Tiffany:

Just hold the towel tight to her head when they come in here and try to get her to stop bleeding.

Matt:

Here, Rebecca, you hold this towel for awhile. I don't want the police to see me sitting here.

Bonnie:

We are in so much trouble. I think I'm going to be sick.

Kevin:

Shut up.

Matt:

I wish I had stayed back with Jeff.

John:

Don't we all.

From *Drama That Delivers*. © 1996. Teacher Ideas Press. (800) 237-6124.

QUESTIONS FOR DISCUSSION

1. Name five consequences of the actions of the students in this play. What do you think will happen now?

2. Have you ever been in this type of pressure situation? How did you handle it? What could Jeff have done differently? What could the others have done differently?

3. Since Janelle did not want to go, what could she have done to get out of it?

4. What happened to all the kids when Janelle got hurt? What was their first reaction? What would you do?

5. When kids are drinking beer illegally in a house, what can happen to the owners of the house?

6. Why didn't any of the students mention the fact that the beer was stolen?

RECOMMENDED READINGS

Fiction

Bunting, Eve. *Jumping the Nail.* San Diego: Harcourt Brace Jovanovich, 1991.

Bunting, Eve. *Janet Hamm Needs a Date for the Dance.* New York: Rosen, 1990.

Fox, Paula. *Moonlight Man.* New York: Broadway Press, 1986.

Nonfiction

Kaplan, Leslie S. *Coping with Peer Pressure.* New York: Rosen, 1990.

Landau, Elaine. *Teenagers Talk About School.* Englewood Cliffs, NJ: Messner, 1988.

Scott, Sharon. *Too Smart for Trouble.* Amherst, MA: Human Resource Development Press, 1990.

IDEAS FOR ACTIVITIES

Group Decision Making

Students form groups of five. Distribute to each group one set of situation cards with various peer pressure situations written on each card. Using butcher paper and markers, students write solutions and consequences for each of these situations.

Problem Solving

Using letters from Ann Landers, Dear Abby, or a similar column, students write their own solutions to the problems in the letters. They can type their responses on the computer, so that when they are shared with the class, no one knows who the advice is from.

Critical Thinking

Students list situations they have encountered involving peer pressure and answer the following questions: What decisions did they have to make? What was the outcome?

Community Activity

In groups, students cut out newspaper articles about students involved in a group activity. It could be a positive activity, such as helping in the community, or a negative one. Analyze these articles and predict how the students in each situation may have been affected by peer pressure. The students write their analyses, discuss them in groups, then bring their findings to the class.

Involvement

Peer pressure can be positive. Have students start a counseling group at your school called Peer Mediation. When there is a confrontation between students, peers are brought in to help mediate. This type of program has been tried at many schools. Talk to your school counselors to start one at your school.

Speakers

The best speakers about peer pressure are older students, such as high school students, because middle school students will listen to high school students more than to adults. Many high school students are willing to talk to middle school kids. They can tell them stories about the pressures and the freedoms they will encounter in high school.

Enrichment

In groups of three, students practice various ways of saying no to bad situations. Each group gets cards on which are described various situations. Two students in the group act out the situation, one "actor" applying peer pressure and the other resisting. The third student listens to the skit, then expresses an opinion about what the characters should do. This is an excellent listening exercise. Students then switch places, letting someone else be the mediator and listener. This exercise allows students to weigh both positive and negative consequences of their actions in a particular situation.

History

Describe for your students a time and place in history when a leader had to follow his or her own way and not buckle under peer pressure. For each situation, students answer the following questions: Would a different decision have changed history? How? This activity can be done in groups of five to six.

Video

Many excellent videotapes deal with peer pressure. Students view one or more of these videos, then review the characters' steps in decision making to see how they handled the peer pressure. Students then write their own scripts to videotape or to perform for an area elementary school.

REFERENCES

Booker, Dianna Daniels. *Making Friends with Yourself and Other Strangers.* New York: Messner, 1982.

Cohen, Susan. *Teenage Competition: A Survival Guide.* New York: Evans, 1986.

Merki, Mary Bronson. *Teen Health.* Columbus, OH: Glencoe, 1993.

Rosenberg, Ellen. *Ellen Rosenberg's Growing Up Feeling Good.* New York: Beaufort Books, 1983.

D
R
A
M
A

6

Dating Responsibly

When students think about dating, many words come to mind. These may include parties, fun, love, friendship, excitement, and scary. Our interest in the opposite sex involves all of these, and dating is an important social skill to learn.

Often, there is too much pressure on young people to date at an early age. The best and safest way to begin the dating process is to go out with a group of people of both sexes. Students are less likely to feel awkward when in a group. There are so many fun activities that groups can do: bowling, dancing, skating, going to the movies, or going for a walk are just a few. Sometimes the most fun is watching a movie at a friend's house. Young people have plenty of time to date; there is no need to rush into it.

Two words that young people need to associate with dating are respect and responsibility. As they mature, their feelings for one another can be very strong. If young people feel old enough to date, they need to be responsible enough to make good choices. If they respect the person they are dating, it will be easy for them to make responsible decisions. Inevitably, when people betray their moral standards, then their self-respect suffers along with it.

Many young people hope to improve their self-esteem and image through the person they are dating. This can lead to an overbearing, controlling relationship. Pressure by either partner can become very intense. A teenager is sometimes not ready for the serious commitment his or her steady date may want. Teenagers who date must be aware of the intensity of feelings of the person they are dating.

Dating should be fun for young people. Adolescents want to be accepted and loved, and sometimes they feel that serious dating is the way to achieve that. The following drama deals with dating, relationships, and consequences. Is there too much pressure on young people to date at an early age? Is single dating really necessary in adolescence? Getting to know another person is very complicated, especially when you are a young teenager. The young teens in this play try to live up to the stereotypical dating scene.

TELL HER IT'S TRUE LOVE . . .
AT LEAST 'TIL THE WEEKEND

Nancy Duffy Hery

Building healthy relationships is very important to teenagers. Part of this process is learning how to date responsibly and with respect. At a time when self-esteem is very important, many young people turn to their peers for approval and respect. But self-esteem must come from within and not from a sexual relationship.

Characters:

Nick	Jake	Jeanne
Chris	Jodie	Misty
Matt	Melinda	Brother
Aaron		

Scene 1 **Boys' locker room. Nick, Chris, Matt, Aaron, and Jake are putting on shoes, packing their gym bags.**

Nick:
So, did you get any?

Chris:
Yeah, how far did you get?

Matt:
The way you two were hanging all over each other at the party, I figured you scored all right!

Aaron:
Well, I didn't score, but let's just say I made it to the 5-yard line.

Matt:
Man, she is hot! I suppose it's true love, right Aaron?

Chris:
Yeah, Aaron's in love now. Did you give her the "I love you?" That usually works.

Aaron:
Hey, "I love you" really does work. It was great. It was easy. Tell her she's sexy, beautiful, and then top it off with, "I love you," and you've got it made. They love to hear that!

Nick:
What does she really look like? Is it as good as we think?

Aaron:
Better . . . you know what I mean.

Jake:
Why don't you guys shut up for awhile? I thought you were friends of hers. You all act like her friend in the hall and then you talk garbage about her as soon as you're in the locker room.

Matt:
Oh, listen to Jake. What's the matter, Jake? Did she turn you down?

Chris:
I always knew she was easy. She just puts on that act here at school.

Nick:
I think Jake has a crush on her or somethin'.

Jake:
I happen to be friends with Melinda. I don't think it's cool to discuss her behind her back.

Aaron:
Hey, chill out, will ya? What's your problem? We're just havin' a little fun here. Hey, maybe you got the hots for her!

Jake:
Shut up, Aaron. I gotta go.

Jake walks to the end of the stage.

Chris:
What's the matter with him?

Nick:
Yeah, you'd think we were talkin' about his sister or something.

Aaron:
I don't think he's had a girlfriend in a while. He needs a woman, and he'll be OK. Hey, he can have Melinda when I'm done with her. She's cute, but she's starting to get on my nerves. As soon as you say you'll go out with them, they act like they own you. Hey, I'm gonna try to catch up with Jake. Hey, Jake . . . wait up!

Aaron runs over to Jake. Nick, Chris, and Matt exit.

Jake:
What . . . you're finished running Melinda's name through the mud?

Aaron:
Man, what's wrong with you lately?

Jake:
You, that's what's wrong with me. She's your girlfriend and you tell everyone your private business.

Aaron:
Hey, between you and me, I didn't really score with Melinda. She's a nice girl and doesn't really do all that stuff. I was just trying to play along with the guys. You know how it is. I have an image to uphold.

Jake: (*disgusted*)
No, I don't know. Now everyone thinks Melinda is easy. I'll see ya later.

Jake exits. Aaron follows a few steps behind.

Aaron:
Hey Jake, wait! You can have her now. I'm through with her, anyway. She's getting too possessive. Hey, wait!

Scene 2 **Jodie, Melinda, Jeanne, and Misty are at Melinda's house later that night.**

Jodie:
That Aaron is so cute. What a hunk! You're so lucky to go out with him.

Melinda:
I know. I can't believe he even asks me out. I was nothing before I met him. I love him so much. He's so sincere and always thinking about me. Did you see him in the hall today, how he grabbed me in front of his friends and kissed me?

Jodie:
Yeah, he's always showing off in front of his friends.

Melinda:
No, he's not. He's just showing them I'm his and that he loves me. He and I are going together forever. Have you noticed how many more friends I have now that we're going out?

Jeanne:
Wake up, Melinda. Do you think Aaron wants only one girlfriend?

Misty:
Jodie, why are you so worried about Melinda and Aaron? They're in love.

Jodie:
Because I've got two older brothers and I've heard them talk. Girls who hang all over guys are talked about.

Melinda:
Aaron isn't like that. Everything we do is private and between the two of us.

Jeanne:
Girl, are you stupid or just gullible? Nothing is private here.

Melinda:
He loves me. I'm not worried. I'll prove it to you and call him right now.

Misty:
I wouldn't call him. Didn't you just call him about an hour ago? And didn't he say he was going to be busy tonight?

Melinda:
Yeah, just watch. He said I can call him any time I want. I'll call right now. (*She walks to the phone and dials, then pauses a moment.*) Hello, may I speak to Aaron please?

Brother appears at upper stage, left corner.

Brother:
Just a minute . . . Aaron, it's your girlfriend!

Melinda: (*whispers to her friends*)
He's coming to the phone right now.

Aaron replaces his brother.

Aaron:
Yeah?

Melinda:
Hi, Aaron. I just called to see what you were doing.

Aaron:
Listen, I told you I was really busy tonight. Why do you keep calling me? Can I call you back later?

Melinda:
Sure, I understand. I love you, too.

Aaron:
Bye.

Aaron exits.

Melinda:
He's really busy. He says he loves me and he'll call me later.

Scene 3 **Next day at the roller-skating rink. Jake and Melinda are standing together. Aaron, Nick, Matt, and Chris are standing in a group across from Jake and Melinda.**

Jake:
Hey, Melinda.

Melinda:
Hey, Jake. Is something wrong with Aaron? He said he'd meet me here, and now he's standing over with all his friends, ignoring me.

Jake:
Oh, they're just talking about the football game tomorrow.

Melinda:
Oh, I thought he was ignoring me. I guess I jump to conclusions.

Jake:
Melinda, Aaron's a good friend of mine, and so are you. Why can't you two just go out, have fun, and not be so serious? Aaron hates when you hang on him.

Melinda:
He does not. He loves me. Maybe you don't realize it, but when I am with him I become important. I still can't believe that he goes out with me. I'll do anything to keep him.

Jake:
That's what I was afraid of. You're such a nice girl. Ya know, sometimes when you're hanging all over Aaron, it gives people the wrong impression. You're not doing anything wrong, but you know how people talk.

Melinda:
Like who?

Jake:
Not anyone in particular. I'm just telling you because we are friends. You don't have to do anything stupid for Aaron. He likes you like you are. That's why he asked you out in the first place.

Aaron, Nick, Chris, and Matt approach Jake and Melinda.

Melinda: (*to Jake*)
Here comes Aaron now.

Chris:
Oh, there's the wife, Aaron.

Nick:
Better run over there quick, Aaron.

Matt:
Make sure you don't talk to any other girls, Aaron, or she'll scratch your eyes out.

Aaron:
Shut up.

The boys reach Jake and Melinda.

Melinda:
Hi, Aaron.

Aaron:
Hi.

Chris: (*whispers to Aaron*)
Hey, Aaron, see if you can really score tonight.

Aaron:
I'll sure try. Watch this. Melinda, honey, you are lookin' fine tonight. Oh, baby, I love those jeans. (*grabs her seat*)

Melinda:
Aaron, not here.

Aaron:
Why not? You let me do it anywhere else. (*grabs her again*)

Melinda:
Aaron, stop it. You're embarrassing me.

Aaron:
You know you love it. Come on, I'm just playing. Let's leave this place so you and I can be alone a while.

Melinda:
Oh, Aaron, I'm so glad you want to have some time alone to talk with me.

Melinda and Aaron exit. Jodie and Misty join the group of boys.

Jodie:
Look at the way Aaron looks at Melinda. It's true love.

Matt:
Hey, where are those two going?

Misty:
I think for a walk and to be alone.

Jodie:
I thought she was staying with us.

Chris:
I think Aaron's taking her to his house for some R & R.

Misty:
Rest and relaxation?

Nick:
No, romping and rolling.

Laughter from all the boys.

Jodie:
You guys are such jerks. Why don't you grow up?

Scene 4   Melinda and Aaron are at Aaron's house.

Aaron:
Hey, my parents aren't home. Let's go up to my room.

Melinda:
No, Aaron, it doesn't look right.

Aaron:

Who cares how it looks? I thought you wanted to show me how much you cared for me. Come on. Ya know what? You're getting to be a real drag. Listen, if you and I break up, you're nothing around here. I make you popular.

Melinda:

Aaron, I know that you're really popular, but those are my friends, too. They'll still be my friends. Let's not talk about breaking up. Let's watch TV.

Aaron:

Hey, if you can't prove that you love me, then I think we should break up.

Melinda:

Please don't say that, Aaron. Give me another chance.

Aaron:

This is your chance. Either you come upstairs with me or start walking to the rink.

Melinda: (*crying*)

How can you be so mean to me when you said last night you loved me? If that's how you want it, see you. I guess we never had anything after all.

Aaron:

You're such a sucker. Go back and whine to your friends. Get out of my house and quit your crying. You'll be nothing now that we aren't going out anymore!

Melinda:

I guess I'll just have to see, won't I?

QUESTIONS FOR DISCUSSION

1. In what ways did Aaron not show respect for his girlfriend, Melinda?

2. Is Melinda's self-esteem affected by her boyfriend, Aaron? If so, in what way?

3. Do you think young people feel pressured to have sex at an early age? Why and where does the pressure come from?

4. Do girls and boys tend to show off in front of their friends and brag about their conquests? Give some examples of what they may say.

5. Are the boys and girls in this story like anyone you know? Give an example of things you can relate to.

6. Does the media affect how you treat the opposite sex? Does it affect how you behave when you are on a date?

7. Can you describe a TV commercial that uses sex to sell a product?

8. What are some strategies for dealing with pressure to do things you aren't comfortable doing? How could you use these strategies when you are dating?

RECOMMENDED READINGS

Fiction

Hest, Amy. *Pete and Lilly*. New York: Clarion Books, 1986.

Martin, Ann. *Dawn and the Older Boy*. New York: Scholastic, 1990.

Stine, R. L. *Double Date*. New York: Pocket Books, 1994.

Westwood, Chris. *Shock Waves*. New York: Pocket Books, 1994.

Nonfiction

Booker, Dianna Daniels. *Making Friends with Yourself and Other Strangers*. New York: Messner, 1982.

McClelland, David C. *Development of Social Maturity*. New York: Irvington, 1984.

Varenhorst, Barbara. *Real Friends: Becoming the Friend You'd Like to Have*. New York: Harper and Row, 1983.

IDEAS FOR ACTIVITIES

Speakers

Most communities have a Spouse Abuse, Prevent Teen Dating Violence Abuse, or other referral service that will send a speaker to your class to talk about abusive dating situations. They are usually willing to speak to teenagers because they feel that abusive relationships start in the early dating years.

Cooperative Groups

In small groups, students list the advantages and disadvantages of single dating and group dating. They then discuss their findings with the class.

Language Arts

Each student writes a personal advertisement for the perfect date. It should answer the following questions: What will be expected of the date? What interests or hobbies should the person have? What do you want them to look like? What characteristics or personality traits should he or she have: funny and smart, serious, quiet, fun to be with? Place the ads on the bulletin board.

Critical Thinking

Students interview their grandparents, asking them to describe their first date. Students ask their grandparents about dating practices during their era, then compare those practices to current ones. Students answer the following questions: What might it be like if you were dating when your grandparents were young? What do you think about it?

Community Service

Organize a fund raiser or baby-clothing drive for a school or organization that supports pregnant teenagers or teenage mothers. These groups can always use diapers, baby clothes, and maternity clothes. This can be a year-long project.

Current Events

Many magazine articles discuss young couples who are trying to make it on their own with a new baby. Divide the class into small groups, give each group an article, and have the groups list all the new responsibilities such a couple would share.

Living Skills

In groups of five, students list 10 places they can take a date. First they list 10 places that cost money. Then they list 10 places they can go for free or for a minimal charge. Next the students rate these places in order of which are the most fun to go to as a group.

REFERENCES

Booker, Dianna Daniels. *Making Friends with Yourself and Other Strangers.* New York: Messner, 1982.

Merki, Mary Bronson. *Teen Health.* Columbus, OH: Glencoe, 1993.

Varenhorst, Barbara. *Real Friends: Becoming the Friend You'd Like to Have.* New York: Harper and Row, 1983.

D
R
A
M
A

7
Controlling Anger

Everyone feels anger. However, the way that emotions such as anger are expressed differs from person to person. They can be expressed in either healthy or unhealthy ways, positive or negative ways. One sign of maturity is learning how to control anger.

As students reach adolescence, they should be learning how to express anger in a healthy way. This is a sign of good mental health. This emotional maturity can be a difficult thing to achieve because expressing anger in a healthy way is a skill that takes practice.

Anger can create tension or stress, which produces adrenaline in the body. Adrenaline prepares the body for a fight or flight. However, there are many other options for young people engaged in a conflict besides fighting or running. The following are some suggestions to help students handle anger:

- Leave the area and go by themselves to cool off.

- Count to 10.

- Exercise, which is good for mind and body.

- Wait a day before confronting the anger.

- Do something they enjoy, such as reading, painting, or cooking.

- Go shopping at the mall. For some people this is excellent therapy.

- Call a good friend. Try to talk about this problem or even change the subject until you feel better.

- Visit a close friend.

- Take a nap.

- Take a relaxing bath.

Here are some tips for kids when facing the person with whom they are angry:

- Be sure to talk in a calm, non-accusing voice.

- Give both parties equal time to tell what has happened.

- Make sure that you are ready to discuss the issue that has angered you. If not, wait another day.

It is important to stress to students that anger can hurt their emotional and physical health. Not only is it stressful, but it can raise their blood pressure, cause heart attacks, and give them headaches.

So what can young people do? They can keep a journal of every time that they become very angry. They should record what happens to them, their family, and their health. How does it affect everyone around them? Can you convince your students to try to control their anger and learn how to live with stress in a productive manner?

See how the boys in the play decide to handle their stress and anger. Is it productive to their well-being?

WHY DO I GET SO ANGRY?

Nancy Duffy Hery

All of us have experienced anger. A true sign of maturity is learning how to control anger. There are many different ways to deal with stress, and it takes practice. This story deals with one boy's struggle with his temper and anger.

Characters:

Patty	Tonya	Mike
David Sergio	Duff	PE Teacher
Olga	Mr. Miller	Dean
Ken	Dianne	Counselor

Scene 1   Patty, David, Olga, Ken, Tonya, Duff, Mike, and Dianne are in shop class.

Patty:
What did you decide to make for your project, David?

David:
I thought it would be fun to make a cup out of wood for my Dad.

Patty:
That sounds too hard for me. How far along are you, anyway?

David:
I've got it shaped and ready to drill the center. I'm afraid to drill without Mr. Stanton's help. I worked so hard on this, and I don't want to ruin it when I'm almost done.

Olga:
Hey, Dave, that cup looks really cool.

David:
Thanks, Olga. Do you guys know when Mr. Stanton will be back?

Ken:
I don't know, but this substitute Mr. Miller is an idiot. If he isn't screaming at us, then he's reading the paper.

Tonya:
Look at him now. Oh, no, here he comes. Everyone quit talking.

From *Drama That Delivers*. © 1996. Teacher Ideas Press. (800) 237-6124.

David:
Why should we quit talking? We're all working, and Mr. Stanton told us that as long as we're working, we can talk.

Duff:
I hate that guy. I asked him for help with the table saw yesterday and he told me to shut up and get busy. He's always too busy to help anyone.

David:
I'll see if he can help me drill this cup. The edge will be pretty close, and I don't want it to snap in half. Every time I ask for help he tells me to quit bothering him.

Mr. Miller:
What are you guys doing? You need to get back to work and quit talking. If you quit talking so much, you'd get your projects done.

Duff:
We are working, but we do need some help.

Mr. Miller:
If you had listened when I gave the directions, you wouldn't ask so many dumb questions. This is your project, not mine.

David:
Mr. Miller, I could really use some help drilling this cup. I've worked really hard on it, and I don't want it to break.

Mr. Miller:
Didn't you hear the directions? This is your project, and you need to do all the work yourself.

Dianne:
But, Mr. Stanton always helps us with the equipment. As long as we're doing the work he'll guide us through the hard part.

Olga:
I sure could use some help with this cutting board I'm making.

Mr. Miller:
I am here to supervise. You need to get busy, quit talking, and stop bothering me.

Duff:
Look at that. Yeah, he's really busy. Now he's reading the paper.

David:
I've got to drill this cup today to get a grade. Man, I don't want to screw up on this last step. I've been working on it for four weeks.

Ken:
Do you want me to try? I'm pretty good at drilling.

David:
You don't understand what I need. Since that jerk won't help me, I'll just do it.

Tonya:
Hey, is anybody going to the beach this weekend?

Mike:
I'm going over to Jetty Park, but only if the waves are high enough to surf.

Patty:
I just boogie board. I couldn't get up on a surfboard if my life depended on it.

Dianne:
I hate the beach. Sand everywhere, and even in places I hate to mention.

Mike:
What a baby. That's the best part. Getting out of the water, lying on the beach with no towel, just sand.

Dianne:
You're a sick person, Mike.

Mr. Miller:
You kids need to shut up and get busy.

David: (*screaming and angry*)
GEEZ . . . I can't believe it. I just drilled my cup and ruined it. Look at this piece of trash. It's ruined. I spent four weeks on it and because of that guy it's shot.

Olga:
Calm down, David. Let me see it. Maybe we could fix it.

David:
Give it to me. I've been asking him for help, but he's too busy.

Mike:
Come on, David. Make something else.

David:
Shut up, Mike. (*He picks up the cup and throws it through the window, then starts smashing things on the table.*)

Mr. Miller:
Hey, what's going on over there? Who just broke that window?

David:
It was me. Are you going to do something about it or are you too busy reading your paper? I'm out of this class right now.

Mr. Miller:
You'd better stop right there, Mr. Sergio. You're in big trouble.

David:
Shut up. You never listened to me or helped me before, so why should I listen to you?

Duff:
Come on, David, sit down, you're getting into bigger trouble.

Mr. Miller:
If you walk out that door, you'll be suspended.

David: (*as he's walking out of the class*)
Good!

Scene 2   Next period PE class. Ken, Mike, Duff, and David are lining up for roll call.

Ken:
Here comes David. Man, I can't believe they haven't called him up to the office yet.

Mike:
I couldn't believe how mad he got over a stupid cup.

Duff:
Hey, let's give him a hard time about losing his temper.

Mike:
Hey, David, how's that cup coming along in shop class?

Ken:
Yeah, I heard that you and the sub are real tight now.

Duff:
I can't believe you flipped out over a stupid wooden cup.

David: (*grabs Duff by the shirt and shoves him to the ground*)
Shut up. Why don't you mind your own business?

PE Teacher:
David, what's the problem? Come here. They want to see you in the front office.

David:
Good. Maybe I can go home now.

Scene 3   David and the Dean of Students meet in the dean's office.

Dean:
David Sergio, come on in and sit down.

David:
Yes, sir.

Dean:
David, according to this discipline referral, you threw a cup out a window, yelled at a teacher, and destroyed property in the classroom. These are very serious accusations. I checked your file and this is not the first time you have lost your temper in the classroom. So what happened?

David:
It's true, I broke the window, but you're not hearing the whole story.

Dean:
Let's hear it then. You're in big trouble.

David:
Yeah, I destroyed property, but you've never been in the classroom before. I had been working on a wooden cup for my Dad and needed some help with the drilling. The sub is a jerk and wouldn't even help me with it. I have asked him on many days for help and he's always too busy or reading the paper. I'm sorry I broke the window, I just lost it.

Dean:
I bet you're sorry. What is your problem? You play in the band, get good grades, and the teachers say you're a great kid. How come I see so many referrals involving fighting and screaming?

From *Drama That Delivers*. © 1996. Teacher Ideas Press. (800) 237-6124.

David:
I don't know. I just can't control my anger. I get pushed too far and that's it. I guess it's because we scream a lot at home, too. I really don't mean to do it.

Dean:
You're going to need some help, buddy, because if you don't learn to control your temper you're going to end up in jail, or we'll read about you in the paper.

David:
I'll work on it.

Dean:
Well, for starters, you're going to have to pay for the window you destroyed. Then you'll be suspended for 10 days for destroying school property. We're calling your parents for a conference before you will be allowed to come back to school. We should kick you out of here.

David:
Do we have to have a conference with my parents?

Dean:
It's either that, or you won't be allowed to come back.

David:
What else?

Dean:
When you get back, I'm putting you into a group called *Anger Control*. It's run out of the counseling office. You need help. This is a serious problem for you.

David:
Going to meetings is not going to help me.

Counselor enters the dean's office.

Counselor:
Excuse me, did you want to talk to me?

Dean:
Yes, this is the young man I was talking about. He's committed many offenses at school. Every time he gets mad, he loses control. When he isn't angry, all of his teachers say he is a wonderful student. I want him to join your Anger Control group. Can you arrange that?

Counselor:

Sure. David, I was looking at your file and I think this would be perfect for you. It looks like this has always been a problem for you. Do you think these group sessions would help you?

David:

It sounds stupid to me.

Dean:

Part of your probation will be to go to these classes. You have to go.

Counselor:

David, why don't you give it a shot? This has got to stop. Life is not going to be without stress, and you need to be able to handle it.

David:

I can't believe this.

Dean:

Now, go out into the front office, so that I can call your parents to come and get you.

QUESTIONS FOR DISCUSSION

1. What would you suggest David do to control his anger?

2. What could David have done differently when the teacher wouldn't help him?

3. What do you do when you are angry?

4. How can you avoid violent situations?

5. List five stressful situations.

6. List five ways to handle stress in a positive manner.

    Examples: Go running

    Talk on the phone to a friend

7. How can a counseling group that focuses on dealing with anger help a person?

8. What do peer mediators do to help students who are angry with each other?

RECOMMENDED READINGS

Fiction

Everitt, Betsy. *Mean Soup.* San Diego: Harcourt Brace Jovanovich, 1992.

Greenfield, Eloise. *Koya Delaney and the Good Girl Blues.* New York: Scholastic, 1992.

Knoll, Virginia L. *My Sister, Then and Now.* Minneapolis, MN: Carolrhoda Books, 1992.

Nonfiction

Berger, Gilda. *Violence and the Family.* New York: Franklin Watts, 1990.

Kurland, Morton L. *Coping with Family Violence.* New York: Rosen, 1986.

Landau, Elaine. *Teenagers Talk About School.* Englewood Cliffs, NJ: Messner, 1988.

IDEAS FOR ACTIVITIES

Speakers

Speakers who will discuss violence and controlling one's anger can be engaged through the juvenile court system, through a program called Prevent Teen Violence, through counseling agencies in your town, and through various mental health groups. Speakers who will discuss abusive relationships can be engaged through Spouse Abuse or Date Abuse.

Cooperative Groups

Students form groups of five to six. They list 10 stressful situations, then they list 10 ways to alleviate stress.

Enrichment

For one week students write in a journal whenever they become angry. They then write how they handled their anger and answer the following questions: Was the way they handled their anger positive or negative? Are they over the anger yet? How long did it take?

Current Events

Students cut articles that deal with violence and anger out of magazines and the local newspaper, then answer the following questions: What happened? Could it have been avoided? Did the anger solve anything?

Video

Many excellent videos address the topic of controlling anger. One good one is *Kids Killing Kids, Kids Saving Kids*, which can be obtained free of charge as a community service video at all Blockbuster video stores. The video, directed and produced by Malcolm Jamal Warner, involves real kids and their stories, along with stories reenacted for the screen. It will spark discussion that could last for many days.

Decision Making

This group activity involves role playing. Small groups of students each receive a brief scenario involving fighting or one or two children displaying anger toward others. The groups create two skits with different endings based on the scenario. One ending depicts a positive way to handle anger and one depicts a negative way to handle anger. The groups practice the skit and perform it for the class.

Class Activity

After reading different advice columns, students create their own advice box in the classroom. Students will have a chance to submit short letters about a problem that they may have. The teacher can choose a couple, and students will help to solve them.

Analyze

In small groups, students write down every song that they can think of that involves anger and violence. Students also write down movies that deal with violence. They then analyze why the market is so large for this topic.

School Activity

Most schools have Peer Mediators to work out problems between students. Students themselves sit down with other students and try to mediate between the two groups, instead of having an adult become involved.

REFERENCES

Berger, Gilda. *Violence and the Family.* New York: Franklin Watts, 1990.

Kurland, Morton L. *Coping with Family Violence.* New York: Rosen, 1986.

Laiken, Deidre S., and Alan J. Schneider. *Listen to Me, I'm Angry.* New York: Lothrop, Lee & Shepard, 1980.

DRAMA

8

Sometimes I Feel So Stupid: Special Education

Every child has the right to an education in the United States. It has not always been that way. Not until the mid-nineteenth century were girls and boys allowed to attend school together, and that did not include children with special needs. A child with special challenges was usually hidden from the rest of the children, ignored, and sometimes placed in institutions if the disability was severe. Special education in the mainstream took a strong turn for the better in the 1970s. Now, many children with disabilities attend public schools. It is important to address this in the classroom.

What is the definition of special education? Special education is individualized education for children and youth with special needs. Children in this category include those with mental retardation, visual impairments, learning disabilities, gifted and creative abilities, behavioral disorders, physical disabilities, hearing impairments, and bilingual needs.

To avoid the stereotyping of special education classes, the following play deals with one of the most common needs in special education, learning disabilities. A learning disability is a disability in which the individual possesses average intelligence but is substantially delayed in academic achievement. (This definition may vary from state to state.) This problem can lead children to feel that they are stupid or of below intelligence when they are not. A child with a learning disability does not learn in the same way as the others in the class. There are many strategies used to overcome some of these challenges.

Children with learning disabilities may have difficulty in math but excel in reading. Other children may have problems in writing, but math is easy for them. It all depends on the child. The stereotype of a child that goes to a pull-out class to get help with their studies is one that needs to be addressed in the classroom. A child's self-esteem is directly related to their success in school. If the children and their classmates realize that this disability does not mean that they are dumb, it will make their time in school more rewarding and enjoyable.

The following play, *Why Do I Feel So Stupid?* deals with a group of children who are in a special education class for learning strategies. They talk about their feelings, how others treat them in class, and how it feels to not always know how to answer a question. This play will help rid your students of the stereotype of a learning disabled child.

99

SOMETIMES I FEEL SO STUPID

Nancy Duffy Hery

We have all had the experience that no matter how hard we try, we have trouble understanding the information presented. For most of us, this is infrequent. If you have a learning disability, it may be common. This play deals with students in a learning strategies class, showing how they deal with challenges at school and at home.

Characters:

Mrs. Brown, Teacher	Heidi	Tiffany
Omar	Mr. Larsen,	Mark
Rachel	Assistant Principal	Andrew
Daniel	Jeremy	Katie
Janessa	Victor	

Scene 1   Classroom setting, teacher is taking attendance.

Mrs. Brown:

Does anyone know where Jeremy is?

Omar:

Man, is he in trouble! Mr. Larsen had to come and get him out of Science. He just went nuts in class. He even threw a chair at a kid.

Mrs. Brown:

What happened?

Rachel:

I was sitting near him when it happened. We had to get into groups, and when he was put into Josh Michaelson's group, Josh whispered to his friends, "Oh great, we get the fat retard in our group." Jeremy heard him.

Daniel:

I wish I was there. What happened next?

Omar:

Jeremy jumped out of his chair and just started throwing stuff. He threw his book at Josh and even his chair. It was great. I was hoping he'd start fighting, but Mr. Jacobs grabbed him.

Janessa:

Geez, the one day I have a dentist appointment, all the good stuff happens.

From *Drama That Delivers*. © 1996. Teacher Ideas Press. (800) 237-6124.

Mrs. Brown:

Well, Janessa, I wouldn't exactly call it good. Jeremy is in trouble now, because he didn't control his temper.

Andrew:

I'd like to kick Josh's butt myself. He thinks he's so great.

Heidi:

So many kids in this school think we're stupid because we come to your class. I'm sick of it.

Mr. Larsen, assistant principal, comes into the classroom with Jeremy.

Mr. Larsen:

Mrs. Brown, please excuse Jeremy for being late. He was with me.

Victor:

Way to go Jeremy! Why didn't you punch him?

Jeremy:

I tried to, but Jacob grabbed me from behind.

Tiffany:

Are you getting suspended or Saturday school?

Jeremy:

They're suspending me for three days. So what? I hate being here anyway. I can't wait to quit and get away from here.

Mrs. Brown:

I had planned a mnemonic lesson for today, but I think we need to have a little discussion. And I want everyone to stay awake and pay attention. Let's put the chairs in a circle.

Jeremy:

This sucks! I'm not doing it. Go ahead and suspend me for a couple more days.

Mrs. Brown:

I'll tell you what, Jeremy. I'm going to give you two choices. You can either join the group in the circle, or sit over in that chair and not say a word. If you want to join us, you may.

Jeremy:

Well, that will never happen, so don't worry.

Mrs. Brown:
See ya. Remember, it's your choice. Now that we have the chairs in a circle, let's talk about ourselves for a minute.

Janessa:
Oh no, Mrs. B. is going to work on our self-esteem today.

Mark:
Are we going to do something stupid? I'm not doing it.

Mrs. Brown:
Let's try it first, and then you can decide, OK?

Mark:
OK, but I'm not doing anything dorky.

Andrew:
You're already a dork, so what's the difference?

Mrs. Brown:
And remember the discussion rules, no put-downs.

Katie:
Move. I am not sitting by you.

Victor:
Shut up, I was here first, so you move.

Katie:
You jerk, put my backpack down.

Mrs. Brown:
Are you two through arguing yet so we can move on?

Daniel:
Yeah, didn't you hear Mrs. Brown tell you to shut up?

Mrs. Brown:
Thanks, Daniel, but I'll handle this. Katie and Victor, come and sit by me so you can handle this discussion.

Katie:
See what happened now, Jerk? Now we're both in trouble.

Mrs. Brown:
Guys, girls . . . This is why we need to have a cool-down discussion. You all need to listen. Hopefully, you'll get something out of this.

Rachel:
Can I get a drink before we start?

Mrs. Brown:
No Rachel, you just got here.

Tiffany:
Are we getting report cards today?

Andrew:
Did you see the fight on the bus this morning? There was blood and everything.

Heidi:
Come on, Mrs. B., let's get started.

Mrs. Brown:
Everyone has to say something positive about themselves. It can be anything.

Omar:
This is dumb. Do we have to do this?

Mrs. Brown:
Yes, and Katie is first. Andrew, will you please put down your pencil and listen?

Katie:
I don't have anything positive to say about myself.

Heidi:
Yes, you do, come on.

Katie:
OK, OK, I have nice, thick long hair.

Heidi:
I'm fast in track.

Jeremy:
Compared to what?

Heidi:
Shut up Jeremy, ya loser.

Mrs. Brown:
Jeremy, you made a choice to stay out of the group. No comments, please.

Daniel:
I can jump my three-wheeler.

Tiffany:
I'm friendly.

Mrs. Brown:
These are all great.

Omar:
I can dunk the basketball.

Andrew:
Yeah, from whose ladder? (*said with a smile, as everyone chuckles*)

Victor:
I can cook spaghetti pretty good.

Mark:
I'm so good looking that the women can't stay away from me.

Laughter from class.

Rachel:
Mrs. B., this is embarrassing, but everyone says that I have pretty blue eyes. Mark, will you quit touching me!

Mrs. Brown:
Please don't be embarrassed. You do have pretty eyes. Quit touching her, please. See, now that wasn't so painful. Everybody has something positive to say. Would anyone like to talk about a certain class they are doing well in?

Jeremy:
Yeah, I'm doing great in science. I'm doing so great I don't have to go there for three whole days.

Laughter from class.

Mrs. Brown:
Another word out of you, Jeremy, and you'll be sent out. Either join the group or be quiet.

From *Drama That Delivers*. © 1996. Teacher Ideas Press. (800) 237-6124.

There are no comments. Everyone just sits and stares.

Janessa:
I think that we are all doing well in your class. But I really hate going to my other classes.

Mark:
I like going to PE.

Mrs. Brown:
And why is that, Mark?

Mark:
Because it's fun!

Mrs. Brown:
Are you pretty good in sports, Mark?

Omar:
He got the Presidential Fitness Award this year.

Mrs. Brown:
Good for you. Does anyone else have a favorite class they are doing well in?

Heidi:
I'm doing better in math this semester.

Daniel:
I hate school. I can't wait to quit. (*to Rachel*) Hey, what are you staring at?

Rachel:
Me, too. As soon as I'm 16, I'm going to get my GED.

Mrs. Brown:
I'm glad you said that, because it really opens up my discussion for today. Why do you dislike school so much, Rachel?

Rachel:
Because half the time I can't figure out what's going on, and the teachers talk too fast.

Jeremy:
Can I join the group now?

Mrs. Brown:
Sure, come on in.

From *Drama That Delivers*. © 1996. Teacher Ideas Press. (800) 237-6124.

Katie:
I have such a hard time keeping my notebook organized. Whenever the teacher has a notebook check, mine is a mess. I just can't do it. I hate school, too.

Mrs. Brown:
Well, organizing your notebook takes time, and that's something that I can help you learn to do. Who else is having some problems?

Andrew:
Why do we have to stay in school, anyway? Both of my brothers quit, and they are working construction with my Dad. My Dad didn't finish school, so why do I have to?

Tiffany:
School is so boring. I'd rather be at home or with my friends.

Mrs. Brown:
I'd like to comment on Andrew's statement. Andrew, I think that it is great your brothers are able to work construction with your Dad, but what if they get hurt on the job? Construction work is very difficult to do when you get older. Without a diploma it is hard to get a job. That's the whole basis of this class. I want to help prepare you for the work world.

Tiffany:
Why try, Mrs. B.? Most of us are too dumb to graduate, so we might as well just quit when we can.

Victor:
I don't know about you guys, but I plan on graduating and going to college.

Andrew:
Yeah, right, Victor. Like we're college bound.

Mrs. Brown:
Victor is right. Many universities and junior colleges offer tutoring services, extended time for test taking, support groups, and books on tape.

Daniel:
I didn't know that. I always thought that I was too dumb.

Janessa:
Mrs. B., someone just snaked on me. OK, who was it? I'm sick of you babies in here.

Tiffany:
It's probably Omar. He always snakes on everyone.

Mrs. Brown:
Can I please continue? Whoever is snaking, stop. College isn't for everyone, and in this learning strategy class I'm just trying to help you get ready for whatever you want to do. We are learning how to organize our thoughts, take better notes, and use little clues to help us. This discussion is very helpful to me. Let's get back on track for a minute. Can anyone else share with me some problems they are having in the classroom?

Heidi:
Sometimes the teachers talk too fast in class. I feel like they are speaking another language. If I raise my hand to ask a question, everyone looks at me and I can tell that it makes the teacher mad.

Mark:
I hate writing in class. I can't spell and I have a hard time with sentences.

Mrs. Brown:
We can work on that, Mark. Lots of kids can't spell, and now that we've been working on the computer, you can use the spell check.

Andrew:
I love computer class. It's my favorite.

Janessa:
I do, too. It's not stupid and boring like everything else.

Jeremy:
I just hate every class, so it's pretty equal.

Omar:
Mrs. B., I hate math class. I feel lost in there. I have always felt that way, even in elementary school. I'm always the last one done on everything.

Victor:
You're not kidding. I just fill in anything, so that everyone doesn't think I'm stupid. It's bad enough having to go to a pull-out class like this. It's not that I don't like you, Mrs. B., it's just that kids think you're a retard if you come here.

Tiffany:
It's even worse when we have to read out loud in class. I can't read very fast and everyone fills in the words for me and groans when I try to read. I just pretend I forgot my glasses that day so I don't have to read.

Mrs. Brown:
Remember how I said that having a learning disability means you must learn to adapt and that you are not stupid? If you are not good at taking notes, then you need to become a good listener or even tape the classes. Teachers will let you do that. It may take you twice as long to finish a book, but that's OK. With practice and strategies it will become easier.

Daniel:
I really like this class, but I hate asking questions in other classrooms. The teachers say things like, "Sound it out, Daniel," or "Weren't you listening when I gave directions?" And I really was listening.

Heidi:
That's what all the teachers say, *"You need to pay attention!"* And I am paying attention!

Janessa:
I hate dealing with my Mom. Both of my brothers do well in school, and she just can't believe that I take so long to do homework. It usually ends up a screaming match.

Andrew:
Me, too. At my house my Dad is a math wiz, and he thinks I am just lazy. I really hate it. I wish I could please him.

Mrs. Brown:
I think that your parents are just frustrated and want what is best for you. We can work around some of these problems. That's why we sit in this circle and talk about ourselves. Everyone has something positive about themselves, and everyone has some type of disability. I'm learning disabled when it comes to fixing anything. I had to learn to live with it and adapt to it.

Mark:
I guess you are right. My Mom is learning disabled in the kitchen.

Mrs. Brown:
Have you guys ever seen me draw a picture? I'm an LD artist.

Andrew:
I was glad when the teachers found out in second grade that I had a learning disability, because I thought I was just the stupid one in the bottom reading group.

Mrs. Brown:

That's right. No one in here is stupid. Sometimes having a learning disability makes it rough in the classroom with other students. Some kids are very cruel in what they say to you. I know it makes you mad, but you just have to make the right choice. Ask yourself, do I really want to blow it for one kid, or do I ignore it?

Jeremy:

I say blow it for one kid! Mrs. B., you don't know what it's like out there. Teachers don't hear half of what goes on in the halls or in the room. I am sick of being called stupid and tired of being called fatso. I made the right choice.

Mrs. Brown:

I know it makes you mad, Jeremy, but lots of things make me mad and hurt. You need to learn how to control your anger.

Jeremy:

Why should I?

Mrs. Brown:

Because after you left the room, do you think the kids thought you were any smarter, or did they just say you were a stupid hothead?

Jeremy:

I don't really care, because I know where that kid lives, and I'll get him after school tonight!

Mrs. Brown:

Jeremy is having a problem with this student and class. Can anyone give him suggestions on how to deal with this frustration in a positive manner?

From *Drama That Delivers*. © 1996. Teacher Ideas Press. (800) 237-6124.

QUESTIONS FOR DISCUSSION

1. What are some ways that we can help students who want to quit school?

2. Why does Tiffany pretend to forget her glasses when it is her turn to read out loud in class?

3. Why does school seem boring to so many of the students in the class?

4. Why do some kids like to pick on kids who are in a special class? What would you do?

5. What are some ways to help Jeremy deal with his anger?

   Example: Using humor to make things easier to take.

6. What are some other problems that the students in this class are having?

7. Are the students showing respect for each other?

RECOMMENDED READINGS

Fiction

Barrett, Joyce Durham. *Willie's Not the Hugging Kind.* New York: Harper & Row, 1989.

Christopher, Matt. *Fighting Tackle.* Boston: Little, Brown, 1995.

Dodds, Bill. *My Sister Annie.* Honesdale, PA: Boyds Mills Press, 1993.

Evernden, Margery. *The Kite Song.* New York: Lothrop, Lee & Shepard, 1984.

Krantz, Hazel. *For Love of Jeremy.* New York: Lodestone Books, 1990.

Nonfiction

Cummings, Rhoda Woods, and Gary L. Fisher. *The Survival Guide for Teenagers with LD.* Minneapolis, MN: Free Spirit, 1993.

IDEAS FOR ACTIVITIES

Video

There are many excellent videos available about children and adults in special education. Two excellent choices are *The Hero Who Couldn't Read* (ABC-TV, 1984) and *Read Between the Lines* (ABC Video Enterprises, 1989). Both of these will spark an excellent discussion about special education.

Speakers

Many speakers are available to discuss special education with your class. Whatever the disability, there is usually an organization that will send a speaker to classrooms to talk about the disability. The March of Dimes, Muscular Dystrophy Association, and Multiple Sclerosis Society all have speaker's bureaus. Your local telephone directory lists these organizations and others.

Class Activity

Students spend a day in which everyone has a different disability. It is a good experience for the children to step into others' shoes. Physical disabilities are important to try first. Place some students in wheelchairs, blindfold some of the children, have some students wear ear plugs, have a few children use braces or crutches, do not allow some children to talk, and give still others something very difficult to read that they must try to translate in a short period of time, like a learning disabled child. Scramble some of the words to make it difficult. When done, the children write in a journal their feelings and frustrations.

Critical Thinking Discussion

As a group, students write down all the special needs names and all the stereotypes about people with these needs. Lead a discussion that addresses the following questions: Why do we think like this? What makes us put them into a category? Do we automatically associate physical disabilities with mental disabilities?

Current Events

Students find stories in the local newspaper about people who have met the challenge of a disability. They then write a paragraph summary of their feelings about the article. Students share their paragraphs in a group setting or with the entire class.

History

It has been discovered that many people in history had a disability that sometimes no one was even aware of. Research one and share your findings with the class. An example would be Franklin Delano Roosevelt, president of the United States. He had polio and had to use braces to walk. Many historians also feel that Albert Einstein had difficulty with such language skills as spelling and reading. Talk about famous actors children like, such as Tom Cruise, who is dyslexic.

Community Service

There are many agencies in every area that deal with people with special needs. They would gladly welcome any type of service that your school can provide. Many students like to help with Special Olympics in their area.

REFERENCES

Biklen, D. *Achieving the Complete School: Strategies of Effective Mainstreaming.* New York: Teachers College Press, 1985.

Cummings, Rhoda Woods, and Gary L. Fisher. *The Survival Guide for Teenagers with LD.* Minneapolis, MN: Free Spirit, 1993.

Smith, Deborah Deutsch, and Ruth Luckasson. *Introduction to Special Education, Teaching in an Age of Challenge.* Needham Heights, MA: Simon & Schuster, 1995.

ABOUT THE AUTHOR

Nancy Duffy Hery was born in Duluth, Minnesota. After graduating from the University of Wisconsin, Superior, with a bachelor of science degree in 1977, she taught physical education and health in the state of Florida. Married in 1977 to David Hery, they have two children, Katie and Duffy. In 1987 and 1989, she was named teacher of the year at her school and 1994 Florida Health Teacher of the Year. She is currently a seventh-grade administrator at Discovery Middle School in Orlando, Florida and working on her graduate degree in educational leadership at the University of Central Florida.

Heard About These Books?